AF430373

THE

EVER-EVOLVING

ART OF BALANCE

"This is going to sound trite, but I wish I had access to Connor's book when I started my first business! I particularly liked the underlying thread of how to refocus when it all gets a bit overwhelming. It just goes to show that a Gen Zer can teach a Baby Boomer new tricks." – Cheryl Lampard, Style Matters International

"Reading this book felt like having a conversation with a friend who was not only telling me about the art of balance but actually giving me the tools to have a balanced and successful life. It has helped and inspired me to grow as a person during a period of stress and uncertainty in my life, and I am sure I will keep coming back to this book to regain guidance and motivation as I continue on my leadership journey." – Marena Sanoja, Florida Gulf Coast University Student and Illustrator

"Frank and to the point. Author, Connor Firmender, provides step-by-step guidance for living a well-balanced life in today's frantic business world." – Robert Swensen, Union Savings Bank

"Connor dives deep into his knowledge on living a well-balanced life. The tips, tricks, and life tools in this book will aid the reader in how to improve their life and find balance within." – Jack Hellmer, Florida Gulf Coast University Student and Entrepreneur

"Relatable and motivating! If you are in search of a book that will drive you towards your goals while sounding like a conversation between a trusted friend or close family member, then this work here is what you need. Firmender doesn't mince his words; he provides for you the pragmatic tools when seeking a life of hard-earned success and mindful balance in a voice that belongs in a contemporary setting. Raw, redesigned, and real." – Mathew Reyes, LeaderShape Graduate and Editor

"If you are looking for a wake-up call or just need help finding balance in your everyday life, then this book truly is for you. Connor discusses his experiences from a young age and incorporates key advice that he has used from his role models to help him strive for balance in his life. This book has opened my eyes and showed me what I need to focus on to reach my full potential. I recommend this book to any age group, but I definitely would have wanted this book as a guide through my college career. Enjoy the journey, everyone." – Kyle Williams, Scotlynn USA Division

"Raw and motivating! This book will be perfect for anyone looking for the recipe for a balanced lifestyle in today's world." – Tyler Walton, NCH Healthcare

THE EVER-EVOLVING ART OF BALANCE

SELF-EDUCATION

FOR A WELL-BALANCED LIFE

CONNOR T. FIRMENDER

ISBN: 9798625735599

Imprint: Independently published **by** *Firmender, Connor T.*
Illustrations by Marena Sanoja

The Ever-Evolving Art of Balance:
Self-Education for a Well-Balanced Life

ConnorFirmender.com

DEDICATION

To my dad and my best friend, Wayne Firmender. A man could not ask for a greater father in his life. Thank you for our days of practicing football with the home-made tackling dummy, for our summer wiffleball games where you taught me the concept of "getting under someone's skin" for the excitement of the game, and everything in between.

To my mom, Mary Penn. Your invaluable and endless love has given me more mental strength than you can ever fathom. Thank you for our days of playing Thomas the Train, watching American Idol, our late movie nights with dollar-store candy, and everything in between.

You both have genuinely given me the tools to make something of my life — and I'm grateful to share the lessons learned with those who are willing to listen.

To my grandmother, Anita Penn (1940 – 2020). Grandma, you're the definition of both an angel and a warrior. From our nights of Jeopardy to our piano and swim lessons, thank you for every moment in between. May you rest in paradise with Grandpa.

To the three of you, I love and cherish every second we get to spend together, and everything I do is for you.

To the CEO and Founder of WearThefund, Sam Lewis. You are a brother to me and took me for an invaluable ride along the journey of WTF. Thank you sincerely for your guidance, support, passion, and the world of business to which you exposed me.

To my professor, Annie Stout. You believed in me when I didn't even believe in myself. You shed light on my natural entrepreneurial abilities. You introduced me to Sam Lewis out of all of the students that you could have selected over me. And you brought me into the startup of FGCU's School of Entrepreneurship.

To the five of you, I dedicate this book and much of what I do in life. Thank you from the bottom of my heart.

TABLE OF CONTENTS

Introduction ....(1)

Preface ....(9)

1. Emotional Intelligence ....(15)

2. Internal and External Perspective ....(38)

3. Life's Fundamentals ....(64)

4. Strength Finding and Empowering ....(83)

5. Have a Mission and Vision ....(100)

6. Goal Setting and Achieving ....(112)

7. Prioritization of What's "On Your Plate" ....(131)

8. The Beauty of Delegation ....(147)

9. Execution is the Game ....(168)

10. Consistency is the Currency ....(182)

11. Holding Yourself Accountable At All Times .(199)

12. Coachability and Constructive Criticism .....(215)

13. Integrated Balance – Not 50/50 ....(231)

14. Life Management ....(250)

15. Assessment Examples ....(271)

Acknowledgments ....(275)

THE

EVER-EVOLVING

ART OF BALANCE

THE
GURU

INTRODUCTION

I want to introduce you to someone — Me. You might have noticed by now, but I'm over on your left. Yup, I'm a Guru, and it's nice to meet you. I'll be tagging along with you throughout the book, so don't mind me popping up here and there.

They always say that a good story begins at the very beginning. Well, here's mine.

Growing up, I was always fascinated by the mysterious ways of life. The way life would throw curveball after fastball after changeup. The idea that life is ever-evolving.

I also have always been one to look for the *balance* in life. What to do, how often to do it, where and when, etc. But it didn't take long for me to realize that it's *much* easier said than it is done.

Throughout my life, I had the pleasure of trying many different things, always looking to better myself, and frankly, to win. It's the mindset I naturally possess. Early on in the second grade, I was already doing sudoku, electrical engineering projects, and realized I had a freakishly accurate photo-memory.

My parents also introduced me to athletics at an early age, and as time progressed, I had the opportunity to play just about all sports competitively. Baseball, basketball, soccer, lacrosse, wrestling, football, swimming, etc. Each one instilled a sense of discipline, time management, and leadership, especially football. Football is the sport that I stuck with through high school. Without a doubt, I accredit many of my good qualities to the game.

When I got to college, though, it was time to move onto my career path (which I knew didn't include professional football), and I was so sure that I had it all figured out.

I was going to be a marine biologist. I loved the water, loved to scuba dive, to fish, and had a passion for marine life. That naturally makes me a marine biologist, right? Nope, not even close. Once I got to college, it was apparent — after completely failing my first exam in biology — that I was no scientist, instead a guy who has those various *passions* and *interests*. But, I was no scientist.

So what did I do after moving over 1,000 miles away from my hometown with no family in Florida? I did what I thought was the next best thing.

I enrolled in a Communication degree. The thing is, I don't even think that lasted a few days until my career advisors were encouraging me to take up a more business-centric degree.

So, I then enrolled in the Business Management degree. It aligned with my career path in a very general sense, but frankly, it still wasn't the right degree for me.

One afternoon, walking with my college roommate from our freshman end-of-year finals, I had a new idea — Resort and Hospitality Management. A degree with above a 97% career placement rate at FGCU, and we were in the top region for Hospitality and Tourism in the entire country. Promising, right? Eh, kind of. At least not for me.

After getting fired from two different internships during my sophomore year of college, I knew something just wasn't right. I had spent over a year trying to find the right degree, but none of them was the right fit for me for various reasons.

With that being said, I always like to express to my younger audience that what got me through this confusing time of my life was *flexibility*. I was flexible with myself, with my surroundings, and with my future. I didn't let failure discourage nor hinder my ability to grow as a man, student, nor professionally.

So again, what did I do? I did the *next best thing*. I enrolled in an Intro to Entrepreneurship course for the Spring Semester of my sophomore year. It was within this class that I met Annie Stout, Sam Lewis, and my first business partner, Brenden Kelly.

Annie, who shed light on my natural entrepreneurial abilities. Sam, who took me in as an intern and showed me the ropes of starting a business. Brenden, who agreed to partner up on a business concept he had. From that point forward, everything changed, and I mean *everything*.

In a matter of months, Brenden and I launched a clothing line, and we were selling merchandise left and right, online and on-campus. We were also sponsoring concerts until we realized *we* wanted to *host* the concerts. From there, we molded into an Event and Talent Management company — hosting shows all over Southwest Florida and managing artists who were on MTV.

All while running this startup, I was taking a full course load of five classes at FGCU.

Not only that, but I was introduced to the Entrepreneur program before it was ever launched and eventually was the school's first-ever entrepreneur within their program. A role that I hold close, as it's now one of the fastest-growing programs in the country and the number one entrepreneur program in the state of Florida. But I didn't stop there.

While running the entertainment company and going to school full-time, I also began working full-time for Sam at his social startup — managing a sales and partnership portfolio that ended up bringing in over $1M in revenue under my role.

How did I have the time for all of this, plus taking care of my apartment, myself, a dog, fitness, and social time? It certainly was *not* easy; I'll tell you that. It took focus, discipline, and *balance*. As I pressed through the years and came to my final semester in college, I made some critical decisions about my future.

I decided to step down from my entertainment startup, step down from the social startup, and focus on developing my current day-to-day: Fieldr — a web-based software solution delivering experiential learning opportunities to students and emerging talent to employers. Our online portals allow both college and high school students to engage directly with for-profit and nonprofit businesses.

I birthed the concept in January 2019 and soon brought on a CoFounder/COO, Natalie Finazzo, to drive this startup to success. Since our launch, we've had the pleasure of working with School Districts, Universities, Economic Development Offices, Chambers of Commerce, and big-name employers in the state, including Enterprise Holdings, Scotlynn Logistics, and Lee Health. I'm very thankful to say this startup has exposed me to much more than business, though.

It's exposed me to an industry that makes me feel as though I belong, as though I am wanted and needed — the Education (and Self-Education) Industry. I now sit on a variety of Advisory Boards for School Districts and the FutureMakers Coalition, and I am a Mentor for LeaderShape, Junior Achievement, and NAF Academy.

My form of income through these engagements is the smiles and growth that I see in students and young professionals. Seeing someone recognize their real vision and purpose from within warms my heart and gives me all of the value that I need in return. All of this because I exist to provide opportunities for learning, growth, and significance.

But I've got a long way to go, a very long way. And that is okay because I'm thrilled about the journey, not just the destinations. Join me on *this* journey to understanding the ever-evolving art of balance.

Connor Firmender
Estero, FL
April 21st, 2020

PREFACE

So, you've decided to self-educate yourself through this book. First and foremost, I applaud you and *thank you* for taking the leap with me.

At this very moment, you might be struggling with balancing everything that's going on in your life. Life can get pretty stressful and overwhelming, and sometimes it seems everything is out of place, and nothing is going right. You also might be doing great in life and are just hungry for more; hungry for more knowledge, more structure, and more insights into what *has* worked and what *has not* worked for others.

There are three immediate keynotes that I want to introduce quickly. 1) You need the right mindset; with this book, I encourage you to be open-minded. 2) You need the right tactics and tools; this book will cover many of those. 3) You need to implement what you learn; use this book as a reference even after reading it.

So, who *is* this book for? This book is for students, professionals, and like-minded individuals looking to take life to the next level through strategic and balanced living. This book is also for those who are looking to make a real impact in this world.

I've done my best to bundle up 23 years of failures and successes, messes turned messages, the training that I've been through, seminars that I've attended, life advice from mentors and coaches, and deliver it all to you in 15 chapters — 23 years into a few days of reading.

My mission is to deliver self-education to *you* that *you* can apply to *your* life *today*.

As I've heard Tony Robbins put it, "Momentum is key to life." I hope this book gives you that momentum to get up and get going, or expose you to a whole new way of thinking and approaching life.

Each chapter, beginning with the very first one, is sequential to the next. I've structured it this way for a couple of reasons. Number one, so you can treat this book as a guide to taking the right steps toward a well-balanced life. Number two, so you can leverage this book as a reference point for when you're struggling to find that balance. Flip back to the chapter(s) you might be struggling with in life, give it a read, and kickstart back up.

I've had the pleasure of speaking — and participating in events — with some of the world's greatest leaders. In this book, you'll be fed insights from entrepreneurs representing Fortune 500s, Inc. 5000 Fastest Growing Companies, the renowned Entrepreneurial Operating System, Forbes 40 Under 40, and more. You'll read impactful stories, quotes, and messages from leaders such as Steve Jobs, Thomas Edison, Walt Disney, Conor McGregor, Bruce Lee, Confucius, Denzel Washington, and many more from several fields of expertise. And you'll read direct responses from masterminds like Gary Vaynerchuk and Tony Robbins.

Before publishing this book, 20 amazing people from a wide variety of demographics read it to ensure that the content *you're* about to read is valid.

The methods of self-education nowadays are proving to be the way to live a better, more meaningful life. I hope this book does that for you.

Let's get started.

THE

EVER-EVOLVING

ART OF BALANCE

Chapter One.
Emotional Intelligence

$\mathcal{A}$s Mike Tyson has put it, *"Everyone has a plan until you get punched in the face."* Now, this is true to a certain extent. Sure, most often, a blow to the coconut will shake you up. But one would hope that your plan was strong enough to withstand that initial blow, and to have the willpower in that plan to stand back up if you've been knocked down.

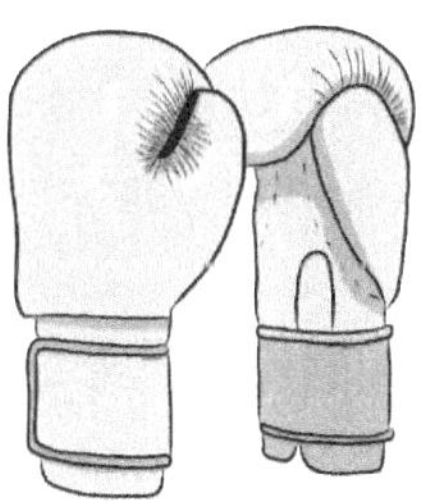

I like to think I'm one of those guys — someone who, no matter what, will pop right back up and hit right back. This has been true in most cases, frankly, just about *all* instances of mine.

But I wanted to start this book with a story where it was difficult for me to stand back up. Not one of us is perfect; let's get that out of the way. Right? I've never met someone perfect — the truth is we're all imperfect in our unique ways.

Now, as cliche as that might sound, it's the truth. We all have stories — successes and failures, laughter and tears — but this is a story of taking that punch to the face and having my plan shaken up, *real* good. And by my plan, I mean my life. This blow *really* shook up my life, and it's undoubtedly an origin to "waking up" — an origin to controlling my internal emotion and my emotional intelligence.

It was August 7th, 2017.
Location: Roatan – an island off of the East coast of Honduras.

Let's lay down the full set. My college roommate, Tyler, and I were on vacation to visit my mom, who was taking a year off from the corporate world (good for her).

We'd been there for two days, enjoying the above 90-degree weather with Pina Coladas, scuba diving in magnificent turquoise waters, and having ourselves a grand ole' time. That is until the evening of the 7th — only our third night.

We had just finished dinner on the beach with some new friends and were heading out for the night to bars and clubs in a separate location about 10 minutes from our resort. Almost too conveniently, we had a rental car to drive; mine, of course. So instead of taking a taxi, we all decided to take the rental.

At around 10:30pm, we departed for the new location. No more than 10 minutes into our drive, my entire life changed.

Now I mentioned it was an above 90-degree island. Well, it had just rained that day as well. What happens when it rains, all while scorchingly hot? The tar oils of the road rise to the surface. Combine that with not much more than a toy rental car, bald tires, rusty brakes, no road signs, no road lights, and an extraordinarily tight downhill turn; you have a recipe for disaster.

As I was coming around this wildly sharp downhill turn, I attempted to engage the brakes...nothing. A moment of dead silence, myself and the three passengers look up, *"oh, sh**."*

Lights. Smoke. Echoes of groans and alarms.

We had collided head-on with a taxi coming around the opposite corner. That vehicle had five total passengers in it. Everyone survived, I'll clarify that right now. Thank God everyone did. But it was close.

Within a few seconds of colliding, my instincts kicked in, and I popped open the door ensuring everyone was okay. They weren't. Especially my roommate, Tyler. He looked at me in confusion, yet thinking he was all right. His face looked as though he was wearing a red mask. A gash on his forehead, deep enough as to where I'm going to leave those details out.

After everyone was rushed to the hospital, the nurses expressed that if I had not pulled off my shirt, closed his head, and held it shut until the ambulance arrived, he would not be with us today. Just writing this breaks my heart to know it was that close of a call.

For this book's sake, I'm going to refrain from getting much deeper into this story. It deserves a book of its own, and you can bet it's on its way.

What I can say, though, is that it did not end there for me. I walked away from the accident with a severe neck injury that the doctors don't expect to ever heal correctly. But I spent the next seven days in Roatan going through something much worse — much more mentally traumatizing.

The night at the hospital, I was awakened by the police with a breathalyzer in my face. The other driver (a local) suspected I had been drinking (I had not) and called them in to question me.

Now, this was roughly seven hours after the accident itself, so it was around 3:30am. I blew. The meter read 999.99%.

You read that correctly, that's not a typo. 999.99% out of a total value of 1,000%. We googled it, anything past about 500%, you're in a legal coma. I was sitting upright seven hours after the accident in a hospital bed with about six different shots and an IV running through me.

Nevertheless, the police officers didn't care. To make a long story short, they attempted to withhold me in a pit, underground. Yes, you read that correctly as well. I ended up having to go to trial, be represented by a lawyer and translator (his 12-year-old son) and was eventually exploited for tens of thousands of dollars.

Throughout the week, I also had a travel ban on my name. I was being held on their island until we coughed up the money.

What a trip.

Yeah, you can say that was a massive punch in the face: *Jab, jab. Right hook.* A *southpaw* from the Notorious and a kick to *you know where*. I was down for the count. This awful experience destroyed any remaining ego that I had about being "invincible." I was not.

My world changed; my view on life changed; my entire perspective changed, and I'm grateful to say now that it's made me a better person.

Again, nobody is perfect. I screwed up, and that was not the first nor only time. But it's events like these that give us the internal strength to rebuild what might be broken and move forward.

Why did I just tell you all of this? This story is similar to many of yours in some weird way. I was vulnerable, I was practically defenseless, and I was exposed to a whole new [third] world.

We have our persona on the outside, and we strive to be the same on the inside, of course. But that internal emotion is what truly defines who we believe ourselves to be.

The internal emotions are the emotions that create the world we live in. They shape our reality and what we perceive it to be. What we believe is right and wrong; what we think feels good and bad. It all originates within your internal emotion.

"Emotional intelligence is the ability to sense, understand, and effectively apply the power and acumen of emotions as a source of human energy, information, connection, and influence." – Robert K. Cooper, Ph.D., Independent Scholar, Leadership Advisor, and Author

When you learn to understand your emotions, you begin to learn how to control them. You learn how to synchronize your outside persona with who you are inside.

I watched a keynote that Will Smith had given, and he was talking about the control of internal emotions and perspective. He said how your world of surroundings is what you've created in your mind with your thoughts and feelings. And when you recognize this direct reflection, you get real careful about how you think and feel.

You begin to realize that you have control over it, you recognize *"I control my thoughts, and I control my emotions."* And when you make that beautiful transformation, everything changes. Your whole world makes a 180, and suddenly what was once bad no longer is. Suddenly, depression and sadness are alleviated, and happiness and peace reside in their place.

When you control your emotions, you elevate your emotional intelligence. When you raise your emotional intelligence, you control your emotions. It goes both ways. And the product of doing so is the control over your life and your surroundings.

For those of you who don't know Tony Robbins, he is an American author, life coach, and philanthropist. Robbins is known for his infomercials, seminars, and self-help books, including the books Unlimited Power and Awaken the Giant Within. In 2015 and 2016, Robbins was listed on the Worth Magazine Power 100 list. He's also six feet and seven inches tall — a powerful guy, no doubt.

Tony has been a business and life coach for experts like Conor McGregor, Oprah Winfrey, Bill Clinton, Leonardo DiCaprio, Hugh Jackman, Serena Williams, and many more significant people.

I had the pleasure and honor of meeting Tony's number one trainer, Stephen Hilgart. Stephen is an awesome guy; he's funny, passionate, friendly, and an all-around great person to work with.

He was giving a keynote at my office in Bonita Springs and was digging deep into internal emotion, emotional intelligence, and the fact that it all begins there — hence why this book starts here with this chapter.

Stephen discussed the importance of focusing on your internal emotion very carefully because it is very much a direct reflection of your reality. Those who allow their negative thoughts or feelings to get the best of themselves will be living a life of pessimism and dragging a metaphorical anchor around their own life.

OPTIMISM V. PESSIMISM

This subsection is straightforward. Being optimistic means you're hopeful and confident in the future being successful. On the other hand, being pessimistic is seeing the worst in things and anticipating a gloomy future. These are directly opposing ways of thinking and identifying your reality.

Who wants to hang around individuals always down and looking at things with a negative mindset? That negative energy wafts right into someone else's life without them even knowing.

I know you've heard this one before — those who you surround yourself with are reflections *of* yourself. If you surround yourself with closed-minded and pessimistic individuals, the chances are you'll carry the same characteristics, and it affects your outlook on life.

You *can* create your reality.

I've noticed the trend is on the rise in our recent generations, and those to come, for recognizing the fact — yes, it's a fact — that you can create your reality. We are at a time when access to near limitless information, data, customers, communities, and everything is at our fingertips.

You do not need a million dollars and an office of employees to change the world. You start by opening a laptop and getting to work.

There's a saying from the almighty sales expert and the real-life Wolf of Wall Street, Jordan Belfort, *"The only thing standing between you and your goals is the bullshit story you keep telling yourself as to why you can't achieve it."* Lose the ego, lose the doubts, and lose the b.s. story that you keep repeating to yourself.

It all begins right within you. To control your emotions effortlessly and build on all of them, you must take accountability for them. Take responsibility for your actions and responsibility for your feelings because your feelings are what caused that action in the first place! Get it yet?

You're in control of your life, so steer the wheel.

Some people are too intimidated to grab it in the first place. Don't be *some* people, be you, and be great at being *you* by taking control of the wheel in your life. This book is here to help you break that barrier and build up the confidence to grip your wheel with an assertion.

As I always like to say, *"Do it with passion, or not at all."* Don't half-ass something because of doubt or call it quits because something didn't work out your way. If everything worked out perfectly and you knew your next day was promised, there would be no room for faith. Faith is at its best when you do not know. And we all need to have faith, no matter our culture or religion. Trust that when you take the step forward or step backward, the wheel is right there, and when you take hold, you will be in control. Faith that *who* you are is exactly who you're *meant* to be.

Believe in yourself and you will be *significant*.

I would say "successful," but someone asked me one day, *"what's the definition of success? What's the metric?"* I thought about it for a second, and I gave him two answers. One of my responses was a handful of the metrics to *my* success. The second was within the context that there is no *one true* definition of success. We all perceive success differently, and that's because we all have our own set of internal emotions. So I say "significant" instead, as much as I can.

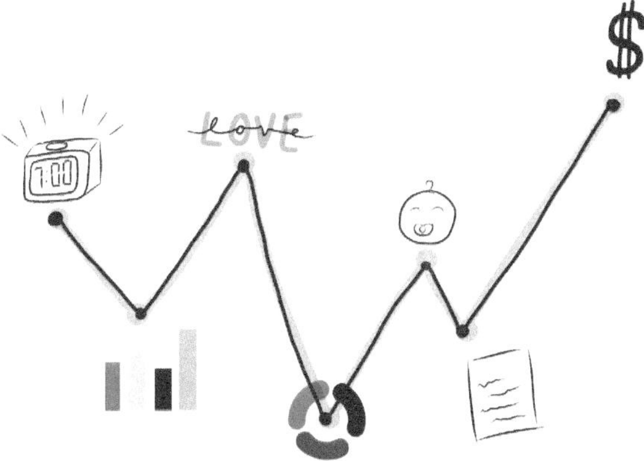

Once you can control your accountability, you'll control what happens next and how you move forward. To tie this all together, holding yourself accountable in terms of your emotions truly just means recognizing what it is you're feeling, why you're feeling that way, and how you can learn from it to be a better you.

Whether you're down on something — maybe you failed a test or didn't get the job you wanted — or happy, it's beneficial to your evolving balance of life to identify what the root of the feeling is, and how you can do better next time.

Not dwelling on what is already down — instead, think forward on what will come of it. What will be learned of it?

Maybe in the case of the failed test, you didn't study wisely, perhaps you crammed in eight hours of studying the day before and thought four hours of sleep and a Bang Energy Drink would get you the grade you're looking for. Most often, this will not result in your favor.

Learn from that. Study sequentially over some time, well ahead of the test date. Watch what you eat, drink water, and create study habitats that remain consistent every time you have a test. You'll build confidence and iterate your test-taking abilities. And get more than eight hours of sleep the night before for heaven's sake (specific context for students).

Or maybe you didn't get that job offer. Perhaps you thought you nailed every single question, had the perfect resume, and wore such a presentable interview outfit. What went wrong? Well, there's always a few reasons. First and foremost, it's likely there was just someone better. So what? Accept it — we all have people more skilled than us at certain things. That's life.

But why was that individual more skilled? Was it your shortage of experience? Maybe instead of getting internships and working while getting the degree, you were at the local beer pong tournaments every week. Look, no hate on beer pong at all, but you must have a balance.

Nowadays, it is a requirement for most degrees to have internships, certifications, and sometimes even training. Speaking to all students, I encourage you to take advantage of as many meaningful opportunities as possible in your community throughout your time in school.

Graduate student, entrepreneur, and a friend of mine, Ashley DeBoer, was kind enough to give us some input on Emotional Intelligence (EQ). Ashley has been studying EQ and organizational behavior most of her life and anticipates her Doctorate being in this subject. If you don't already find her impressive, she's a member of Peace Corps EC91. Talk about a game-changer. I had the chance to ask Ashley, *"How does emotional intelligence relate to great leadership and a well-balanced life?"* Her stellar response:

"When you dissect the four main competencies of Emotional Intelligence: self-awareness, self-management, social awareness, and relationship management, you see how much it filters into our everyday lives. We understand how much EQ impacts who we are and how we perceive others and ourselves. Throughout my life, I've been both a leader and a follower, and when I was choosing to follow, I allowed myself to be led by people I believed in, who exuded passion and values and shared in mutual respect. Now, as I venture further into my professional career as a leader, I understand how enhancing my emotional intelligence has fostered immense personal and professional growth. It has allowed me to make more reliable connections, work through conflicts, and communicate in a way that honors and respects other people's considerations and perspectives.

By being transparent and creating an environment and culture that adapts, achieves, and cares, people are influenced to be better, and that's what great leadership is all about. When I began my journey of personal growth through the enhancement and consciousness of emotional intelligence years ago, I saw every aspect of my life transform as I learned how to handle conflicts sooner rather than later, how to talk about my feelings and expectations, and how to be more empathetic to others on their journey. Overall, it has encouraged more genuine and authentic relationships in all facets of my life, and I have learned that when you have people in your corner who are dependable and ambitious, anything is possible." – Ashley DeBoer, Author, Entrepreneur, Blogger, and Traveler

What I genuinely appreciate about Ashley's response is her self-awareness of the impact that EQ had on her growth. She refers to the enhancement and conscious effort she put into strengthening her EQ, and in doing, she has been triumphant in her pursuits. It has allowed her to make reliable connections, work effectively through conflict, and foster the ability to communicate inclusively.

INTERNAL BEHAVIOR

Self-care.

There is such a lack of focus on self-care, and I often see it in the entrepreneurial world. You must take good care of yourself. Period. The younger you can start, the better.

The way we treat our health is the catalyst for poor internal behavior. By definition, *internal states* are behaviors that are maintained by consequences domestic to the person. Just in case there is any confusion, these are the negative thoughts that emotionally affect us inside — the depressive state and uncontrollable anxiety.

Dr. Neal Barnard is the founder of the Physicians Committee for Responsible Medicine. He is an advocate for plant-based nutrition, ethical research, and medical training.

I want to point out the plant-based part. Barnard gave a terrific keynote at the VegFest in Bonita Springs in February 2020, and he was discussing a story of a few patients he had a few years ago.

Unfortunately, one patient was dealing with anxiety and depression, and was looking to be put on medication. Dr. Barnard encouraged his patient to go on a plant-based restricted diet for six weeks, and in the end, he would analyze the results.

What do you think happened? If you said to yourself something along the lines of *"a plant-based diet replaced the anxiety and depression with appreciation and happiness,"* then you're right. After six weeks, the patient reported minimal to no symptoms of previous anxiety and depression.

Nutrition is not the only essential ingredient in stable mental health; physical activity is also a priority. Doctors recommend exercising at least three times per week. Many people will excuse their lack of physical activity with a busy schedule, but we all know it's laziness and an inability to manage time.

We'll get into all of that throughout this book. Especially time management.

One activity that has seemed to work for many, including myself, is meditation. I'm meeting more and more people, friends alike, who meditate regularly. I like to start my mornings with a short period of five minutes of meditation, and I'll typically meditate as the final part of my day, ultimately carrying myself into a beautiful night of rest.

I did some statistical research into the relativity between physical fitness and mental health, and quickly found some evidence relating to my position. In 2018, the US National Library of Medicine: National Institutes for Health put together a report on *"The relationship between physical inactivity and mental wellbeing: Findings from a gamification-based community-wide physical activity intervention."* The abstract of this article says enough.

"Abstract: Mental health accounts for 13 percent of the total global disease burden with predictions that depression alone will be the leading cause of disease burden globally by 2030. Poor mental health is consistently associated with deprivation, low income, unemployment, poor education, poorer physical health, and increased health-risk behavior. A plethora of research has examined the relationship between physical activity and mental wellbeing; however, the influence of community-wide gamification-based physical activity interventions on mental wellbeing, to the authors' knowledge, is yet to be explored. In view of this paucity of attention, the current study examined the relationship between physical activity and mental wellbeing pre/post a community-wide, gamification-based intervention. The findings revealed that increases in mental wellbeing were significantly greater for the least active prior to the intervention, and a strong, positive correlation between the increase in physical activity and increase in mental wellbeing was observed" (ncbi.nlm.nih.gov/pmc/articles/PMC5774736/).

So what does this all mean? There is a ton of research continuously being conducted on the correlation between mental health and physical activity.

Towards the end of the abstract, we see that current findings have revealed a strong and positive correlation between physical activity (i.e., lifting weights, cardio, HIIT workouts, calisthenics, sports, etc.) and the improvement in mental wellbeing.

I also want to mention hygiene being relative to mental wellbeing and EQ; a few obvious but necessary measures include dental, and cleansing your body, hands, face, and hair frequently! Again, all obvious, but all necessities in sustainable mental wellbeing.

Make the time for it.

Take care of your body, and your body will take care of you. Make an effort to exercise at least three times per week. Your health will thank you for it and so will your family.

This doesn't stop at meditation or physical exercise, and not even with hygiene. But that should go without saying. Take care of your body — your skin, your teeth, your everything. It all will play a role in the emotions you feel internally.

Three takeaways: external is a direct reflection of internal, prioritize your self-care, and when situations seem cynical, it is because you're carrying a negative presence and emotion into it. Reflect on that, and you'll almost always find it correct.

SELF ASSESSMENTS

Write down one to three things you're grateful for every morning, or every other day, and genuinely mean it — repeat daily for at least 90 days (Ch. 15 Example A).

"I don't want to be at the mercy of my emotions. I want to use them, to enjoy them, and to dominate them."
– Oscar Wilde, Irish Poet and Playwright

Wilde's expression of using his emotions, enjoying them, and dominating them all relates to what we're discussing throughout this entire chapter.

When your emotions are identified, you're able to use that to your power and control; you're ready to create *your* reality and paint *your* picture.

Not only that, but enjoy those emotions that you're feeling. And dominate them — another synonymous word for "control."

Having control over one's own emotions allows for greater control of a balanced life. Controlling your feelings puts your entire life in your hands — or should I say the steering wheel is in the palm of your hands.

You begin to ride the terrain of life and find your balance as you take days head-on. At that moment, life is in balance, and it is beautiful.

When you've identified what you're made of and what kind of emotions your life draws from you, then the ability to balance it all becomes seamless.

WRITE SOME NOTES

Take this opportunity to jot down a few thoughts that might be going on in your head. How are you feeling right now? Hopefully, what I've been discussing related to internal emotion and emotional intelligence has resonated with you. Treat this as your journal or use it as a reference guide to your EQ.

____

____

____

____

____

____

____

____

____

Emotional intelligence relates to one's perspective. We've discussed this a bit already, but in the next chapter, we'll dig deep into internal and external perspectives. Into the relativity between attitude and emotion, and the "world's mirror."

Chapter Two.
Internal and External Perspective

$\mathcal{A}$s we briefly discussed in the first chapter of this book, perspective plays a significant role in your emotional intelligence.

Just as emotion lives internally and externally, perspective does the same — hence the title of *this* chapter. But what exactly do I mean by this? *Internal and External Perspective? "Elaborate, Connor."* You got it.

The way you feel inside is the origin of your perspective; stabilize your foundation, and your viewpoint will stabilize.

To elaborate and simplify, the way you feel inside towards something, someone, or well, anything, is your perspective. And those emotions are the origin; the reasons as to why that's the way you "see" or perceive something.

It's the way you define, identify, feel about something. Many synonymic words can be used, but for our time in this book, we'll use perspective (or perceive). We'll go a bit deeper into that. We'll define how exactly your perspective relates to your reality and relates to your balance. Let's begin.

A perspective *will* change the way you think, the way you look at life, and your purpose. First and foremost, having a stable attitude is extremely important. And frankly, this also means having those internal emotions under control and aligned with yourself in your entirety. Your perspective will not only originate from how you feel but it truly then defines how you think — your mindset altogether.

Let's break down a story to exemplify the power of perspective — Inky Johnson, a former University of Tennessee defensive cornerback. Now, he is a renowned motivational speaker.

Inky's football career ended in 2006 when he awkwardly and devastatingly took a hit from an opposing player. Inky was rushed to the hospital, where he was facing a life or death situation.

The hit had caused internal bleeding in his chest, and the doctors had to rush him into emergency surgery to plug the main artery from his left leg into his chest. Inky tells the story of when he woke up to the doctor standing over him, post-surgery, *"He had good news, and he had bad news."*

The good news is that they had saved Inky's life. The bad news, he suffered severe nerve damage in his right shoulder. He would never be able to play the game of football again.

In Inky's speech — one he gives many times over across the United States — he brings tears to one's eye.

"No way. No disrespect to you, Doc, but I've been working for this since I was seven years old. No disrespect to you, Doc, but you weren't in the park with me and my mother when I was seven years old and she was sitting in that Buick Regal after she got done working at Wendy's. No disrespect to you, Doc, but you didn't come up in that two-bedroom home with 14 people sleeping on the floor. No disrespect to you, Doc, but you didn't miss those meals and stayed focused and never made an excuse. I never cheated!" – Inky Johnson, Motivational Speaker and Former College Football Player

Inky fought through adversity. Inky became exactly who he set out to be at a young age, challenging himself day in and day out to become one of NCAA's best cornerbacks and well on the way to the NFL. But from one wrong hit in a game, it was all taken away.

Now, this is where the average is separated from the significant. Inky could have given up and fallen back in life — sulking in his tragedy. A life-long worth of work, just gone. It sounds pretty rough to me. But Inky didn't let this adversity stop him from being heard. He didn't just turn over and allow this to hinder his ability to make a difference and pursue something he loves.

Not long after his accident, Inky became an inspirational speaker and traveled the country speaking for large audiences of students and professionals. He's turned his life into a mission to spread messages of perseverance and instill ethics of hard work, passion, and determination.

This perspective that Inky had about his accident, his life, and his future was so healthy that he'd built a world where he still plays the primary role in his outcome. The perspective that despite life-altering adversity, life is still very much worth living to the greatest of your effort and ability. The attitude that we're all given *one* life, so live it — no matter *what* and *who* tries to prevent you.

Although I cannot relate in the same context, I see eye to eye with Inky. I see eye to eye in the sense that life will be unfair, and it will be cruel, but in the same darkness, there can be light. And that light is your perspective.

Have the power to adjust perspective.

It takes practice and consistency. Now a more practical situation might be the loss of a job (maybe you got fired), or perhaps life just does not seem to be going your way at all. It feels like everyone is out to get you sometimes — or all of the time. Maybe you just don't feel like what you're doing is working.

Let's start with the job. I'm a firm believer in opportunities presenting themselves in what are seemingly failures.

Your loss of the job could be because you genuinely are just not inclined to that position. But not to worry! This is the opportunity to take a leap at a new position that maybe you've always wanted to try but were too secure with this previous job.

And on that note, let me take a quick second to implore you to pursue something that you're incredibly passionate about. As Steve Jobs said, *"People say you've got to have a lot of passion in what you're doing, and it's totally true. And the reason is, it's so hard, and any rational person would give up."* Although in the context of starting your own company — which I also implore you to do too — this can be relative to your life altogether. *Do what you love, and you'll love what you do.* That's one of my mantras. That, and *live with purpose, love with passion.* Another thing I implore you to do; have personal mantras to live by.

Now, back to the point of perspective. As I said, you're back on the job market. Find what you're passionate about, what you love to do, and pursue that new opportunity! Even if it's in the same industry or the same area of location, just any change is good. And that's the perspective you've got to have on it.

A pioneer of Estero, Florida, by the name of Nolen Rollins, told me that all great leaders *manage* change. Well, that begins with controlling your perspective on the move itself.

Now let's say you just think life is ultimately going against you. I'm here to tell you that it is, in fact, *not.* Life is just unfair to all of us — but that's okay. That's what makes life so exciting and keeps you on your toes; it's always changing, and efforts to balance are ever-evolving. After all, balance *is* an art form.

What might sccm to bc going wrong, is genuinely the Universe's work of placing you on the right paths, and it's best not to fight it. Explore. Be open-minded. Be a forward thinker. The less resistant you are to this crazy changing world, the more effective your ability to balance will be, and the more in-control your perspective is.

Practice this perspective.

And by that, I mean pay attention to it. Monitor how your mindset is at certain times and with certain people. The more self-aware you are, the more you'll understand how to control that perspective.

I encourage you to put effort into that adjustment if you're feeling the world is against you, or things are all going south. Manage that change, have faith there is light at the end of the tunnel, and you will find your feet.

Not saying it's easy, so it *does* take effort to control emotions, which do naturally control perspective. Of course, it's always easier said than done. But again, that is why I encourage you to put in the effort to monitor those emotions and perspectives. It will make the adjustment and controllability all the more effective.

Our friend Inky didn't wake up the next morning a motivational speaker — at least not as far as I'm aware. It took time, acceptance of the situation, and a lot of heartbreak, I'm sure. But through determination — the determination he speaks on nowadays — Inky controlled his perspective and turned his life into something even more impactful to his community and supporters. We all have it in us, just dig deep and it's there.

Just like everything, you get out of life what you put in, but be patient. What we see that goes on around us is a reflection of everything we've been discussing. I've said that a few times now, and you'll hear me say it more throughout this book. It all begins with the internal.

Renowned actor and movie producer, Clint Eastwood, has even been quoted to say, *"What you put into life is what you get out of it."* The efforts that you put forth in all of this change and your control will reflect the progress and outcome that you receive.

If you don't even bother monitoring your perceptions and don't care to understand why your life is going "against you," you are certainly not going to get the outcome you genuinely wish to see. You will not see and feel the progress you sincerely hope to achieve. You are your own competition at the end of the day, so act like it and become a better version of yourself every day.

I mentioned I'd be touching on the art of reflection more. Well, we're back! Allow me to reiterate if you don't quite understand it yet.

Changing your perspective will change your surroundings. And frankly, it goes both ways. If you change your surroundings, you're more empowered to change your perspective. But let me be clear about this. You cannot just run from your problems and hope those new surroundings will make everything grand and perfect. It does not work like that. You must always focus on controlling that perspective because then, once you do, you can place yourself anywhere on a map and be happy. *But,* yes, changing your surroundings — whether that be who you surround yourself with or the places you frequent — can and will affect perspective.

While I was still in high school, I started getting into quite a bit of trouble; I was hanging around some of the wrong people and the wrong type of influences. In the blink of an eye, I was making terrible decisions, and I had carried this narrow-minded perspective that led me into a depressive mindset.

It lasted for a year or so until I started changing my surroundings and who I surrounded myself with. Life then got brighter; my narrow mind opened up, and everything I chose to surround myself with offered a sense of growth.

As time went on and I got to college, this same concept remained valid. When I would stop going places that did no good for me, my intimacy with life grew stronger; my perspective grew healthier.

Give it a try!

Start with one specific thing going on in your life — it may be a toxic relationship, maybe you're not doing too well in school, or not loving your job. Start monitoring what it is you feel and why you think that way at those exact times.

Ask yourself, *"Why?"* five times until you've dug deep into that perspective's root. I promise you answers are lying beneath as to why you perceive that way and what it is you need to do to feel more optimistic like we talked about earlier.

I bet in a matter of days or weeks, you'll begin to notice some incredible changes and new feelings going on. The sun will start to shine a bit brighter, the grass a bit greener, everyone is a bit friendlier than before. And sequentially, as you begin to expand the control across your entire perspective, then you'll see there's a whole new world on the other side, and you're on the way to it.

Sign up for DailyOm emails.

Head over to *https://www.dailyom.com/* and subscribe for free. Let me be upfront and say this is *not* an advertisement at all. I've been signed up for years now, and these emails have changed my life.

You will receive emails daily of self-encouraging, improvement, and insightful messages that honestly have been relative to my life nearly every single time.

Give this a try, and I promise that if you do read the emails, you will see the change start to impact you *and* your life. It's crazy how relevant these emails will be to what I'm trying to control or make better at that exact time. Anyway, let's take a look at some more examples of self-assessments.

SELF ASSESSMENTS

Break down all of the "bad" things occurring in your life. Write them down. Dig deep as to why these things are bothering you and what a possible solution might be. Identify one silver lining. Practice accepting what is and focus on what can be done (Ch. 15 Example B).

"In the middle of difficulty lies opportunity." – Albert Einstein, Ph.D., Theoretical Physicist; Theory of Relativity

This quote is all about perspective. And we mentioned something very similar earlier in this chapter. In the middle of difficulty, failure, and adversity, there are plenty of opportunities awaiting you.

Whether it be the opportunity for learning and growth or the opportunity for change, it is, in fact, an opportunity. You must treat the situation as so. If one dwells on the negativity and sulks in sadness, then the chances of recognizing opportunities are slim.

Again, you get out what you put in. Put in the effort of recognizing opportunities. Albert Einstein and I can assure you it's there. I've failed many times over and over, but I've learned to appreciate these failures, and so every time I trip up now, it's just another reason I'm able to move forward more productively. Listen to Albert and recognize the opportunity in difficult times.

Be accepting of what *can't* be changed.

"Well, Connor, what you're saying is so much easier said than done. What if things are just out of my control?" If something is just out of your control — and unless you're willing to start an initiative that would pursue legal change — then move forward! Move onward! There is no reason or point in exerting your precious time and valuable brainpower on something that is just out of your control.

Some people just get overly consumed in placing their efforts and emotions into a trend in life that their perspective becomes so narrow-minded. Narrow-minded thinking is the last type of thinking you want to have. You'll miss so many precious opportunities as they fly right by your face, while you've got your binoculars laser-focused on the ground. Open those eyes and open your mind up.

A terrific book I would recommend related to our discussion is *"The Subtle Art of Not Giving A F**K: A Counterintuitive Approach to Living a Good Life"* by Mark Manson. Trust me, it will change your life. It will open your eyes and mind, and then you'll begin to select very carefully where you give your "fucks" (time, money, effort, etc.).

"You and everyone you know are going to be dead soon. And in the short amount of time between here and there, you have a limited amount of fucks to give. Very few, in fact. And if you go around giving a fuck about everything and everyone without conscious thought or choice—well, then you're going to get fucked." – Mark Manson, Best-Selling Author and Blogger

We're also limited to the number of good (quality) decisions per day; don't waste your decisions (decision fatigue). Amazon Founder and CEO, Jeff Bezos, is what most people would consider a genius. One of Jeff's most critical pieces of advice relates to the number of decisions one should make in a day. His suggestion, *three* impactful decisions per day.

Sure, you have to make a handful of other smaller, somewhat daily repetitive decisions that become more habitual but do your best to limit yourself to three *impactful* decisions. This is according to the world's richest man, not just me.

Frankly, this piece of advice has helped me tremendously. Once I was able to stabilize my schedule and limit myself to a lower amount of core decisions per day, my days became more powerful and progressive. So did my weeks and months.

Rather than checking off a ton of things just for the satisfaction of achievement, I focused on things that would advance me another level forward. I was no longer trying to run two different companies, while responsible for a third while trying to start another endeavor while juggling chainsaws (kidding). I did the wise thing, stepped down from one startup, parted ways with the third company, restricted my new endeavor to monthly instead of weekly, and felt the relief of unnecessary fatigue.

In other words, quality over quantity, my friends. There truly is something called *decision fatigue*, which is when you're exerting your thoughts and precious brainpower by overloading your plate and mind with too many decisions to make. It also suggests that your quality of decisions decreases as the day goes on and with the more decisions you make. All in all, do your best to focus on quality over quantity when making decisions.

Sometimes it takes a life-altering moment to put your reality into perspective; your reality is not everyone's, so don't be fooled.

What I'm referring to is that very moment in your life when you realized you're not superhuman, and you are very much bendable — not breakable — but bendable.

One of *my* moments was the story of Roatan, Honduras. That week's experience surely put my reality into perspective. I was a privileged American in a third-world country who had just screwed up big time by crashing a car and now at the control of their government. What a situation.

But all moments are different. Some include the passing of a relative, maybe the near-death experience when you were young, or the toxic relationship you tried excusing for too long.

The point is that sometimes it takes this type of life event for someone to have their reality put into perspective. That's when life changes.

Another way to look at this keynote is more positively. Your reality is not everyone's reality of you, so don't be fooled. In fact, many people will paint their own picture of you and who you are. Some allow moments to define their image of you, others your story, others your personality. From mistakes made at a young age to embarrassing moments in your young adult life and poor decisions that a "drunk you" might have made, people can be relentless in the picture that they paint, and you should feel sorry for them. Because at the end of the day, nobody knows *you* like *you*. You know yourself more than anyone, so protect that at all times and stay true to that person who you know you are. Don't be fooled by the pictures painted or things said; those are temporary. *You,* my friend, are permanent.

Your *legacy* is permanent.

ABSORB KNOWLEDGE AND INFORMATION

You choose what to believe. Choose wisely.

At this point in the book, you might think I'm a bit crazy. Well, you might just flat-out know it, which I'm cool with. Maybe some of the keynotes I've discussed aren't something you can entirely agree with. And that's okay because self-awareness is powerful.

After all, nobody knows you like you, so I'm not here to define you nor tell you what you must believe. I just hope that what you choose to think and apply is positively impactful on your life.

This goes for everything. You choose what to believe and apply to your life, so choose wisely because it will be the reflection in the mirror. You become what you think and wholeheartedly feel.

Be a sponge. Be a forever learner.

Think of the most influential person in your life right now, or even the multiple people. I can promise you that these men and women are students themselves. And no, I don't specifically mean a student at a formal institution. I mean a *learner*, someone who is constantly absorbing information and amplifying their knowledge.

You never want to be the smartest person in the room, never. Always be surrounding yourself with people who naturally make you a better *you*, people who impose goodwill and experience on you. There's no better self-education than expertise from someone who's been through what you're going through.

Experience is key.

And the experience is a teacher in itself. So to that, I say always be a student. Always be a learner. Always be someone who feeds on knowledge and never is too full for more.

You can be like most corporate CEO's and read an average of 52 books per year, or maybe you're someone who loves podcasts because you learn best from listening. Or perhaps you're someone who is just all about hands-on. Well, whatever the case may be, put in that effort and see your return.

Warren Buffet, the former richest man in the world but still a top contender, has suggested investing mostly into personal knowledge throughout your 20's. For my readers above the age of 30, I think we can agree this concept still applies. Invest time, money, your resources into learning new things, expanding your knowledge, your brainpower.

Those who continue to learn will forever hold the upper hand on society; stay one step ahead or at least keep up. As I mentioned that your influencers are students of their own, well, that is the reason they are who they are. They never stop learning; they never stop bettering themselves day in and day out. And because of that perspective on life, to be a forever learner, they've become the person you instantly thought of in your head moments ago.

Now, I'm not telling you to read a hundred books on financial intelligence and then you'll be the next Buffet, but what I'm saying is those who continue to learn will forever hold the upper hand on society.

Leading up to this book, I knew that I wanted to bring outside contributors' perspective — credible professionals in a variety of industries and fields of expertise. Of these many contributors is an exceptional colleague of mine and someone I consider a friend — Dr. Christopher Blakely. Currently the Director for FGCU's Multicultural Leadership Development office, Dr. Blakely is heavily involved in the higher education industry and is passionate about serving young professionals. I asked Dr. Blakely, *"How does internal and external perspective relate to our ability to live a well-balanced life?"* and I couldn't have asked for a better response.

"At the beginning of writing this, I stood amidst an opportunity to serve as Interim Director for a department, in addition to my current role as director of a separate unit. This appointment was both exciting and validating. Although it would be an interim role, I was appreciative of the opportunity to apply my experience, insight, and perspective to this new role and serve the staff of this area.

Before accepting this appointment, it was vital for me to discuss it with my wife, family, and personal advisory board. As an ascending student affairs professional, work-life balance has long been a priority for me. Being a husband and father has always been set at the apex of daily living.

Shortly after working in higher education, I came to discover that my personal success and happiness was less about work-life balance, but predicated more on work-life integration. As one who is fortunate to work in a passion area, the work is less of hard work and more of heart work. Therefore, working extended hours or going above and beyond job duties was not particularly draining physically, but I quickly recognized if I continued down this route, it could impact what I have placed at the forefront of everything, family.

When we think about the adage to never get so busy making a living that we forget to make a life, I recognized that it would be critical to shifting my perspective. My perspective changed from less of developing work-life balance and more of creating work-life integration. Generally, when we consider the balance between work and life, we often associate this stability by giving portions of ourselves to both entities. However, this approach can be limiting. Through the process of integrating my work with my life, I have come closer to establishing a harmonious whole.

Bringing one's whole self is critical in being fully present, maintaining authenticity, and maintaining a proper perspective. Shifting my perspective allowed me to think not on what position I wanted to obtain, but consider what problems I sought to solve. This has helped guide my growth towards what I need to learn to be able to solve problems, rather than who I want to work for.

In 2018, Disney released 'A Wrinkle in Time' directed by Ava DuVernay based on the science fantasy novel of the same name. A young girl on a quest to find her missing father is joined by three special celestial travelers Mrs. Which, Mrs. Whatsit, and Mrs. Who.

Mrs. Who generally speaks in quotations from famous thinkers and writers as she found it difficult to form her own sentences. One quote in particular from Mrs. Who, 'I don't understand it any more than you do, but one thing I've learned is that you don't have to understand things for them to be.'

As we seek to navigate life, two truths that I have discovered, is if we can master balance and perspective, we can find freedom and peace. We must recognize that balance does not equate to being 50/50, but rather correct proportions of steadiness. Like riding a bicycle, for one to keep their balance, one must keep moving. Additionally, success in life can be associated with one's perspective. It's you against you every day, and it is vital to make sure you win. The mind is everything; what one thinks, one becomes, therefore, our real power rests in the mastering of self. Six plus three equals nine, but so does five plus four. The way one perceives something is not always the only way. Be encouraged to respect varying perspectives of thinking while maintaining balance." – Christopher W. Blakely, Ed.D., Program Director, Speaker, Mentor, and Entrepreneur

Viewpoint on the outside world sheds light on the weight of your life and the appropriate balance.

This perspective that we've been discussing all chapter long, it's an animal in itself as you can tell. And it takes some taming to stabilize it and create the world you want. To create the reality that you envision — *your* reality.

This mindset sheds light on your life; it sheds light on what needs to be balanced. You see opportunity; you see the world the way you want to view it. And with the effort that you put in, you see the results. This all plays a role in that masterful balance ability.

WRITE SOME NOTES

Take *this opportunity* to jot down some thoughts about your perspective. Have you been feeling out of place and wondering why? Or maybe just struggling with seeing clearly. Let it all spill on this page to help untangle everything. Ask yourself, *"Why?"* five times to dig deep on your perspective.

Perspective relates to life's fundamentals. Now that we've covered some significant keynotes that begin our journey to balancing life — internal emotion, emotional intelligence, and internal and external perspectives — let's dive into life's fundamentals.

As much as I believe a lot of this all starts with the first two chapters, this next chapter stabs at something many people struggle with and have mixed emotions about — life's fundamentals.

Onward we go.

Chapter Three.
Life's Fundamentals

Like I've repeated a few times now, it all begins with *you*. More specifically, though, it starts with you at home.

In this seemingly obvious yet massively important chapter, we are going to review some fundamentals of life. These fundamentals are the core to your wellbeing, your ability to do absolutely anything [good], and are simply the root of the success in balance that you seek.

It's so easy to lose focus and prioritization of the fundamentals of life. Before jumping right into the three core fundamentals, let's make this clear. These are going to come across as *"duh, why are we even spending time talking about this?"* But if you begin to feel that way, then I encourage you to open up your mind to possibilities and hold yourself accountable for everything we discuss in this chapter.

It is very, very easy to lose focus and stability in your fundamentals of life. In fact, after years of participating in various leadership forums, committees, and so forth, I've discovered that a root — if not *the* source — to my colleague's pains comes down to their fundamentals. Well, the lack thereof.

We've lost sense of nature yet need Vitamin D.

In other words, we all lost a sense of the world we live in! When the internet was launched and email became a norm, the web was a new world for everyone to escape to. Nowadays, it's the opposite, and the internet is our reality while the natural world is where we escape to. It's funny how history will evolve and pull a 180 on itself.

I know I've been guilty of not getting outside quite enough — spending all day in an office, hunched over, destroying my posture. Or just on the couch with Netflix on and Instagram being opened every five minutes to see if anything new has been posted when I know I just checked it minutes ago. It's almost like a habit. Well, that's because it is.

We've created a world of virtual reality and a natural world of rarity. As a software startup founder, I have plenty of advocacy for the use of technology and the difference it has made — but that's another time and another book. For now, reference *"Zero to One"* by Peter Thiel if you want excellent insight into technological advancements and the reality that it's all created as well as what our future holds.

To sum up my point here, get outside more! Go for a run, a walk, do some social media posting outside if you need to combine the two due to necessary time consolidation. But just build it into your schedule (more to come on this later in the book) and stick to it.

For months now, I've been able to cut out enough time in my schedule to take my workouts outside. After my lifting session, I'll grab my cleats and head over to a nearby field where I'm regularly doing cardio and other active drills for footwork technique.

Everyone is different, though, so take this concept of building more time in the natural world and apply it to what works best for *you,* even if that means running around the blocks in your concrete jungle for all my city people! Just make it work — it's on you.

Okay, so now that I've laid down the ground here for these fundamentals, let's dive right into what they are!

SLEEP

We'll start here. Let me tell you something about sleep. We've seen all of these motivational posts on social media about how *"only the rich are willing to sacrifice sleep"* or *"if you want to be successful, you can only*

sleep five hours a night." I'm here to tell you that it is all b.s.

We need the proper amount of sleep, period. The adequate amount of sleep allows us to function at our most impactful day in and day out. It's what will give you the ability to perform at your best day in and day out. The proper amount of sleep is what drives a healthy body, inside and out.

You see, these individuals that claim they can thrive off minimal sleep every night are either lying to feel superior or yet to run into the wall of exertion.

Now doctors have even tested and proven the results behind getting a proper amount of sleep, which for humans is roughly between seven and nine hours per night. So what makes these people think they're above science? You've got me beat. Ego, I would have to say. Beyond that, some are just new to their path and only recently began trying to sleep minimally every night. At one point, I was one of those people.

Throughout my junior and senior year at college, I was sleeping roughly four to five hours per night, and what I thought to be performing at my best each day. I was taking five classes (approximately 20 hours per week), working a full-time job developing a small business (roughly 60 or more hours per week), as well as starting up my first company in the entertainment industry (approximately 20 hours per week). And you can imagine the entertainment startup kept me up during after-hours.

So, while I was a student in college, a mere 19 to 21 years of age, I was putting in about 100 hours per week into my endeavors. Factor in time to breathe, eat, stare at a wall for a couple of minutes, and you're not left with a whole lot of "week." I was hardly sleeping. I was in bed at or by 2am and then up again around 6am to 7am. Sometimes I just didn't sleep because we were hosting a show that night.

I tried doing this for those two years consistently, and let me tell you something; it caught up. I began noticing my mental stability crumbling, my health deteriorating, lost about 20lbs, and had never been that light in weight since my freshman year of high school.

This schedule depleted me, and I've seen the same in countless peers, friends, and colleagues. This lack of proper sleep profoundly affects our decision-making abilities as well. We discussed decision fatigue earlier in this book — well, the lack of sleep is one of the leading causes of decision fatigue.

Just as Jeff Bezos, Amazon Founder and CEO, suggested limiting yourself to three core decisions per day, Jeff is also an advocate for the proper amount of sleep. For getting your eight hours. He has once been quoted claiming he does not use an alarm clock. Instead, he allows his body to awaken when it is naturally ready. Now, this might not work for everyone, after all, Jeff is a rare character himself altogether, but it is the concept that matters. Your body needs the proper sleep — give it to yourself, and you will see all the difference in your day-to-day.

"It's not about how much sleep you get, it's about what you do when you're awake." – Gary Vaynerchuk, Entrepreneur, Author, Speaker, and Social Media Expert

NUTRITION

This subsection heavily ties into my story of when I was in college. You see, my body also lost so much weight because I did not appropriately feed myself the right amount of nutrition. My first meal would often be around eight o'clock at night, along with my first cup of water. I would just be so consumed in my work that I'd forget to eat and drink. My lack of sleep played a huge role in this inability to recognize my nutritional needs.

But even if you're getting your three, or maybe two, full meals per day, it's *what* you're consuming that truly matters. Are your breakfasts bacon or sugar cereal? Lunch, a small microwavable plastic dish of mush? How many bags of chips and fruit snacks a day?

Look, I'm not here to call you out, but then again, I am if that's what I need to do to open your eyes. Although these foods might make you feel full, your body is often not receiving the proper nutritional value it requires. Add this to the lack of sleep, and you've got yourself a recipe for lower energy, performance, clarity, and many other results that you don't want to feel.

Now I'm not one of those who agree that just stopping "cold-turkey" can work efficiently. Most often, that method does not work because you haven't allowed for a transitional period between the changes. So, treat this in moderation. Start substituting certain produce for ones of less sugar, plant-based, or even just organic. Start removing one sweet snack from the grocery list every time you shop, until you have almost none or none at all. I promise you healthy foods can be very tasty — just get creative, but more importantly, just get started.

Ever since I have made the leap to a plant-based diet, my body has felt like that of a charged-up Tesla Model S P100D (look it up). And ever since I've been getting my seven to nine hours of sleep every night, my body has felt like a king's. These two fundamentals are undoubtedly two of the most important things to focus on in your life to achieve the balance you seek.

But there's one more fundamental that we cannot leave out.

LOVE

Once you take care of yourself, you will respect yourself. When you find yourself, you find love.

Once again, it starts with you, with *you* loving *yourself*. Not partially, not slightly, nor *only* something about yourself. Loving yourself in your entirety. Loving your imperfections; your unique physical, emotional, and spiritual attributes.

Everything about you was created as so for a reason — a much higher reason than you can ever imagine, but it is your responsibility to believe who you are is exactly who you're meant to be.

By the end of this book, I want you to be able to stare at yourself in the mirror — unless you already do — with a smile of confidence, true belief in yourself, and the love that you feel for yourself.

Once you wholeheartedly love yourself, I promise that you'll then find you have limitless love to give others. People feed off of self-love and confidence, especially in leaders. When an individual can stand up tall and firmly speak his/her belief, there will always be an audience willing to hear and follow in his/her confidence.

I want to take this moment to bring up a great concept a mentor once taught me, and I've been grateful to share it with many peers of mine who have gone on to see success in the changes they made. *The empty bucket concept.*

You see, everyone has a bucket; mine might be striped blue and yours polka-dotted, but we've all got one. And in that bucket is what we can give others, especially the love we have to offer.

Now, if you continue just to give and give from your bucket without pouring in more yourself, then you'll soon find an empty bucket in your hand with nothing left to give. *"Wait, Connor, won't other people be filling my bucket while I fill theirs?"* We all hope so, but we can only believe. We cannot expect that everyone who receives what we have to offer, or anyone at all for this matter, will be giving in to our bucket. Do not give with expectation; give because it is the right thing to do. *"So, Connor, who fills up my bucket consistently so I'll never run out of giving?"* If you're thinking to yourself *"me,"* then you're right. It's *you.* You're responsible for ensuring your bucket is full of love, energy, willingness, and ability to give. While you're giving relentlessly without expectation, your bucket has remained full of self-love and confidence. And this, ladies and gentlemen, is a concept that has shed light on the importance of loving yourself and ensuring you are accountable for your bucket.

"Thousands of candles can be lit from a single candle, and the life of the candle will not be shortened. Happiness never decreases by being shared." – Buddha, Philosopher, Mendicant, Meditator, Spiritual Teacher, and Religious Leader

All of the above in this chapter, and frankly just about all that we have already discussed in this book, can heavily relate to Abraham Maslow's Hierarchy of Needs. Centuries ago, Maslow had created this order of human needs to sustain life — deficiency needs and growth needs. The five pillars are as follows:

"Maslow (1943, 1954) stated that people are motivated to achieve certain needs and that some needs take precedence over others. Our most basic need is for physical survival, and this will be the first thing that motivates our behavior. Once that level is fulfilled, the next level up is what drives us, and so on.

1. Physiological needs — these are biological requirements for human survival, e.g., air, food, drink, shelter, clothing, warmth, sex, sleep. If these needs are not satisfied, the human body cannot function optimally. Maslow considered physiological needs the most important as all the other needs become secondary until these needs are met.

2. Safety needs — protection from elements, security, order, law, stability, freedom from fear.

3. Love and belongingness needs — after physiological and safety needs have been fulfilled, the third level of human needs is social and involves feelings of belongingness. The need for interpersonal relationships motivates behavior. Examples include friendship, intimacy, trust, and acceptance, receiving and giving affection and love. Affiliating, being part of a group (family, friends, work).

4. Esteem needs — which Maslow classified into two categories: (i) esteem for oneself (dignity, achievement, mastery, independence) and (ii) the desire for reputation or respect from others (e.g., status, prestige). Maslow indicated that the need for respect or reputation is most important for children and adolescents and precedes real self-esteem or dignity.

5. Self-actualization needs — realizing personal potential, self-fulfillment, seeking personal growth, and peak experiences. A desire 'to become everything one is capable of becoming' (Maslow, 1987, p. 64)" (https://www.simplypsychology.org/maslow.html; https://www.verywellmind.com/what-is-maslows-hierarchy-of-needs-4136760).

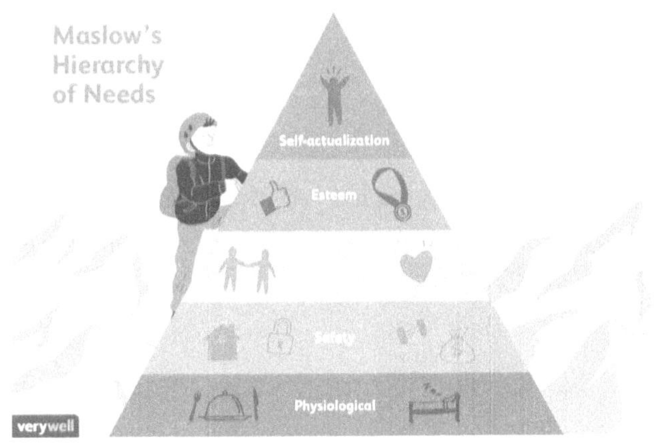

SELF ASSESSMENTS

For 26 days straight, stick to a proper sleep schedule, eating schedule, and cutting out time for family, friends, and alone (Ch. 15 Example C).

"Success is neither magical nor mysterious. Success is the natural consequence of consistently applying the basic fundamentals." – Jim Rohn, Entrepreneur, Author, and Motivational Speaker

Earlier in this chapter, I mentioned that I find people frequently struggling with their work due to this lack of focus on fundamentals. From business owners and CEOs to executives to dishwashers at the local bar, this lack is shared among everyone and is often ignored.

It's often disregarded due to ego or denial. Some just have awful time management skills and don't feel they have time for a "real meal" or time to get proper sleep, and that's nonsense. Everyone has the time; it's what you choose to do with it.

"The successful warrior is the average man, with laser-like focus." – Bruce Lee, Actor, Director, Martial Artist, and Philosopher

In other words, you don't need to be some outlier of expertise or power. All you need to be successful and a warrior in life is to be highly focused. Our three fundamentals play an essential role in your ability to focus, and the more focused you are on sustainable fundamentals, the more focused you'll be in life altogether.

Common myths.

"Food is food," "No need for sleep," "I'll rest when I'm dead," "I don't need me-time" … you guessed it, more b.s.

These are all egotistical phrases that have stuck around for the sole purpose of feeling superior. When in reality, we all need sleep. Sure, you're going to rest when you're dead, which may be a bit sooner than you want because guess what, your health is deteriorating and you've got a heart attack coming on a Monday afternoon before the age of 65. You don't need me-time? I certainly don't want to be there when you explode in front of your colleagues or family from overexertion and mental stress that you refuse to relieve.

Ladies and gentlemen, do not let these common myths feed into your ego. You need proper sleep. You need adequate nutrition. And you need love.

Time management is a venue.

Build a schedule; it's not that hard! If you're the type that struggles with staying true to your plan, then maybe it'd be wise to bring a friend or colleague into the situation. Someone who can casually, and without much effort, ensure that you're staying on schedule and call you out when you're not. Some people call this an "accountabillibuddy," a buddy who holds you account-able. These are people you want to keep close. But I'm getting ahead of myself already, so again, more to come on this later.

At my church, I had the pleasure of being introduced to a young gentleman by the name of Brandon Catron. Brandon and I share a lot of commonalities when it comes to leadership, athletics, and overall life. I look up to him.

A preacher, Beachbody Coach, husband, father of three, and fellow former football player. He's got a lot on his plate at all times, and when you've got three little ones running around all of the time, it can get to be a bit overwhelming. Brandon was kind enough to share some insight for us on life's fundamentals. I asked Brandon, *"How do these fundamentals (sleep, nutrition, and love) relate to one's ability to balance life and everything in it?"* His response:

"I find myself running on empty when I do not prioritize fueling myself with what my body is lacking. When I am in-tune with my body, then I can diagnose what it needs. But to be able to diagnose what my body is requiring properly, I must love it. I must cherish it. It is through loving the temple that was given to me by God that I can fuel it with the most effective nutrients needed. When I fuel it properly, I can go into idle for a given number of hours to recharge and get through the next day. I cannot expect to move through the day at max capacity if I have not planned time of rest and a time to prepare my food for that day. Plan for the future by preparing for the present." – Brandon Catron, Preacher and Coach

Lockdown your fundamentals, and balance will come much more straightforward. By focusing on these three fundamentals that we've discussed throughout this chapter, I promise your ability to balance life will come so much easier — a world's amount easier.

It is all too common for people to lack the proper amount of sleep per night, lack the appropriate nutritional value in their diet, or just lack love for themselves and therefore lack love for their surroundings.

Lockdown these fundamentals with the right amount of sleep by building it into your schedule — get yourself a white noise machine if that helps you to fall asleep quicker — and the right amount of healthy foods as well as consistent love and support for yourself.

WRITE SOME NOTES

As we've done in the first two chapters, take this moment now to write down a few notes about your thoughts on fundamentals.

Are you getting the right amount of sleep? Do you need to stop working so late at night and know when to call it a day? Maybe you want to write down some ideas of new grocery items to try the next time you shop. Let the brainpower flow.

Ever-Evolving Art of Balance

Fundamentals relate to strength finding. Okay, so now we've covered three keynotes of the origin to balancing life — emotional intelligence, perspective, and fundamentals.

As we progress through this book, these next five chapters will focus on some key tactics and traits of successful people. All information and advice that I've learned over the years from entrepreneurs, executives, professors, and inspirational leaders alike.

Let's go!

Chapter Four.
Strength Finding and Empowering

$\mathcal{U}$nderstanding common strengths is near effortless. Identifying *your* real strengths is a process. Especially when you don't quite have any methods set in place to self-assess. I'll be sure to review some techniques that are proven to not only help identify your strengths but also validate them.

In this chapter, we're going to discuss strength finding and empowering those strengths to become a better *you*.

Let's begin!

First and foremost, we want you to know your strengths as soon as possible. The earlier the age, the better. Once you've been able to identify what they are, you're ready to apply them in the necessary forms.

By that, you'll have clarity on what you can be highly successful at, where it ought to be done, who to do it with, when to do it, and how exactly it will be done. Notice something? Knowing your strengths allows for clarity on the five "W's" and the one "H." Who, what, when, where, why, and how. Having this knowledge truly makes all the difference when moving through life. It clarifies your mission and vision (we'll discuss these in the next chapter). The earlier you can find purpose and form that mission and vision, the further you'll go. I'm not saying it's a race, but you also don't want to be moving through life aimlessly without a sense of what it is you're highly capable of achieving.

Explore activities and hobbies — experience. Do things, try things, explore ideas. And let's also clarify this goes for any age, not just the younger age ranges. At whatever point in your life you are at right now, there is always more to go and more to learn about yourself. And if you happen to be saying to yourself right now, *"Well, I'm not young anymore, so this isn't relevant,"* then all I have to say is being young is a mindset. Be grateful for the amount of time you do have left and understand that it is always better late than never.

Experience, altogether, is what exposes you to challenges, to "new," and all of this sheds light on what you're naturally skilled at — what your strengths are. Most successful people possess this ability and can identify what their variety of concentrations are, most likely younger than others. In the long run, this is what gave them the upper hand to those who were late to discover their strengths.

A bit further into this chapter, I'll reveal a handful of "celebrities" or well-known people who have been doing what they do since they could practically crawl.

But first, we're going to take a left turn and dive into identifying weaknesses. Believe it or not, this plays a massive role in your ability to determine your strengths.

IDENTIFYING WEAKNESSES

Understand that weakness is healthy and needed. As I'm writing this right now, I almost want to say that the only "person" who possesses no flaw is an extraordinary piece of new-age AI (artificial intelligence). But even then, that machine would itself possess weakness. For example, it most likely couldn't configure and troubleshoot a toilet or offer heartfelt empathy to divorcing couples. So I guess it's safe to say everything and absolutely everything possesses weaknesses.

Identifying that at an early age is just as beneficial as identifying your strengths early on. But let me be clear here, what is once a weakness *does* have the potential of growing and becoming a strength of yours. It's just most often not going to be as strong as your natural strengths.

Identifying these weaknesses offers you the opportunity to build on what is minimal, a chance to become a better you by focusing on that weakness and stabilizing it.

What are *my* weaknesses? I have so many!

I'm not quite empathetic by nature, and that's certainly something I've been working on. I'm not the greatest with money management, so that's *most definitely* what I'm working on. Another weakness, I'm a terrible billiards player — you'll never catch me at a casino.

I accept this, which allows for my decision making and team building to be very successful. I implore you to ask yourself what your weaknesses are — what your weakest link within yourself is. You'll have space at the end of this chapter to jot some notes down again.

Once you've gotten these weaknesses down, accept it with pride! It's one thing to say it aloud and feels good that you've been honest with yourself. But it's another when you truly accept it for what it is and then can delegate effectively; build ideas and teams around yourself to accomplish much more. We'll dig deep into delegation in a few chapters — we're getting there!

Be proud of what you're weak at. I know it sounds contradictory, but this clarity and confidence in who you are at your entirety will allow you to build 10x! Shoutout to Grant Cardone. Be proud of those weaknesses! And then do something about them if you so choose.

SELF ASSESSMENTS

Gallup StrengthFinder 2.0™ and DISC Analysis. (Citations, Online).

"Nothing can be more absurd than the practice that prevails in our country of men and women not following the same pursuits with all their strength and with one mind, for thus, the state instead of being whole is reduced to half." – Plato, Philosopher and Pioneer of Higher Education

For my friends who took a philosophy course in college, does this sort of quote sound familiar? I certainly recall a whole semester, or a few, with elaborative discussion and readings on Plato, Aristotle, and Socrates. As Plato puts it, there is nothing more absurd, or wildly unreasonable, than the practice of men and women who are not following their strengths in their pursuits. Simply put, people are wasting valuable time when they're heavily pursuing something that is not of their skillset or abilities. And the consequence for this lack of direction is minimal progress, living half of the life they're meant to, and living imbalanced.

Break down your strengths and analyze them.

The reason you're able to live a well-balanced life through the identification of your strengths is that you're going to apply them to everyday life and your goals.

Let's take a few specific strengths — three to be exact — from the Gallup Strengthsfinder Assessment. After taking the assessment, I was able to identify my top three strengths, which are Achiever, Futuristic, and Activator. According to the StrengthFinder 2.0 Book written by Don Clifton, these three strengths break down as follows, beginning with Achiever.

"Your Achiever theme helps explain your drive. Achiever describes a constant need for achievement. You feel as if every day starts at zero. By the end of the day, you must achieve something tangible in order to feel good about yourself. And by 'every day' you mean every single day — workdays, weekends, and vacations" (Strengthsfinder 2.0 From Gallup, By Tom Rath, 2017, page 37).

This identity could not be any more true about me. Since I've been able to identify this, I've been able to direct my days in a very strategic manner, ensuring what I'm getting down is, in fact, productive, tangible, and benefits not only myself but other people. Next one — Futuristic.

"You are the kind of person who loves to peer over the horizon. The future fascinates you. As if it were projected on the wall, you see in detail what the future might hold, and this detailed picture keeps pulling you forward into tomorrow" (Strengthsfinder 2.0 From Gallup, By Tom Rath, 2017, page 105).

This, again, could not be any more true. Since a very young age, I have always been one to think ahead — into the future. What could be? What can be done to evolve? It's a critical skill as a serial entrepreneur. The third one — Activator.

"'When can we start?' This is a recurring question in your life. You are impatient for action. You may concede that analysis has its uses or debate and discussion can occasionally yield some valuable insights, but deep down you know that only action is real. Only action can make things happen" (Strengthsfinder 2.0 From Gallup, By Tom Rath, 2017, page 41).

And of course, spot on.

So what are your strengths? How do your strengths help you grow and achieve your goals? Knowing your strengths allows you to understand what to apply to the day-to-day operations of your life. Ultimately, you become the best version of yourself, all while being confident in every move you make.

Some other strengths identified in the Strengths-Finder 2.0 book include Adaptability, Competition, Command, Developer, Empathy, Includer, Positivity, Strategic, and Woo. Yes, Woo.

I reached out to Gary Vaynerchuk for a brief statement to include in this book. His response falls significantly in line with this chapter. Gary responded, *"Being the bigger person and having empathy and humility for the other person is a strength and often the answer to the situation. It takes confidence and caring to be able to do it. Try it. Practice it. Get comfortable with it!"*

WORKING SMART, NOT JUST HARD

Always work smarter and strategically, not just harder. At the end of the day, when you've identified your strengths and identified your weaknesses, it all comes down to how you apply it in life. Always be working in strategic ways to ensure you're not overexerting your energy and brainpower. Ensure you're still getting the proper sleep, nutrition, and love.

And the reason you'll be able to do so, effectively, is because of how strategic you'll be in your day-to-day life. You're making those three core decisions, applying what you're highly skilled at to higher risk and reward activity, and delegating your weak links to a team.

It's an old cliche, but most definitely work smarter and strategically than just harder. I remember hearing this phrase one time at a business conference, *"Work smarter AND harder."* I agree — work smarter than the competition and work harder than the competition; it goes both ways. But frankly, that hard work — that progressive work — will be the product of smart work.

Exhaustion is natural; the smarter that one can work, the more progress will be seen. Throughout the book, we've discussed that overexertion is real, and it begins with you at home (i.e., fundamentals). So the more productive you want to be, and the more progressive you want to be will originate from the smart and strategic application of information we've been reviewing.

Be a hybrid of the tortoise and the hare, quickly progressive with stability and consistent forward movement. Nobody said the hops had to be a hundred feet high or long.

This concept — my hybrid animal creature — is entirely made up by me, and I hope you like it!

So, a *hybrid tortoise/hare*. *"What on Earth is that, man?"* What I mean by this relates to the classic tale of the race between the tortoise and the hare. The story ends in the tortoise winning because it was slow and steady; it was consistent throughout the race. While the hare was moving fast as he launched, he stopped to hang out because it was so far ahead, or so it thought. The tortoise eventually wins the race because of its slow and steady pace.

I'm here to tell you to be a hybrid.

Move fast, take advantage of your strengths like we've been discussing; use those strengths to your advantage, just like a hare is fast and speedy. But the key is to remain consistent, remain steady.

If moving fast will throw you off balance, then it is best to remain slow and steady, and that's perfectly fine. That'd be a strength for you to identify that you work better slowly and steadily, so keep at it. If you're someone like myself who needs to be moving fast and consistently see tangible progress every day, then leverage that strength and just be sure to progress steadily. Be a hybrid between both, and this involves identifying those strengths and weaknesses.

I mentioned we'd look at some celebs who found their calling at a young age. Well, here they are.

CELEBRITY EXAMPLES

Athletics.

Serena Williams is an Olympic tennis player who revolutionized the sport, winning more Grand Slam singles titles (23) than anyone else during the open era. Serena has been ranked number one in many categories, beginning her career at the age of three.

Kobe Bryant (Rest In Paradise) was a professional basketball player. As a shooting guard, Bryant entered the NBA directly from high school and played his entire professional career with the Los Angeles Lakers, winning five title championships. Kobe started playing the game of basketball when he was also three years old.

Tech.

William Henry Gates III, better known as Bill Gates, is a business magnate, software developer, investor, and philanthropist. He is best known as the cofounder of Microsoft Corporation. By the age of 13, Bill was working on computers and bartered free access to his school's computer lab in exchange for developing their software. For some great information about Gates' success from a young age and the origin of his story, read *"Outliers"* by Malcolm Gladwell.

The list can go on and on. Sure these are icons of their industry, but they got there somehow. And I can promise it was not because they just moved through life without direction and sense of ability. Not at all, rather the complete opposite.

They recognized their natural skillsets, knew their strengths, and turned into the best version of themselves, ultimately evolving into one of the best to do it.

"I really think a champion is defined not by their wins but how they can recover when they fall." – Serena Williams, Olympic Tennis Player

These individuals identified their strengths at an early age and applied the majority, if not all, of their time, effort, and consistency to those strengths until they became the very best at what they did.

Nobody will pay much for a lot that is *kind of* good. They'll spend a lot on a little that is *astounding*. Jack of all trades most rarely is a master of one.

Knowing what you're good at and not good at puts you in the driver seat of a balanced life. It might sound redundant at this point, but you have to identify those strengths and weaknesses to know what you're good at and what you're not so good at.

This ultimate clarity will enable you to balance your life and everything that is in it. If you don't even know what it is you're skilled at, then you've been balancing the wrong things this entire time, and it's hindered your progress.

WRITE SOME NOTES

This chapter took a stab at you. I know. Again, I'm not here to call you out, *but* then again I am if that's what's needed.

Take this moment to jot down what you've identified as strengths and weaknesses, and next to them, write down how they apply to your day-to-day. Maybe you'll come to realize you're doing all of the wrong things. Laying this out on paper will give you a visual and sense of direction.

____

____

____

____

____

____

____

____

____

____

____

____

____

____

____

____

____

____

____

____

____

As we wrap up this chapter on strength finding and empowering to become the best version of yourself, I hope you've been able to see your life a bit clearer, and maybe this book has sparked a new inspiration for change and growth.

In this next chapter, we'll dive deeper into specific methods and ways for you to make the practical application of this content into your life.

Up next, having a mission and vision, and the active pursuit of them.

Chapter Five.
Have a Mission and Vision

Claiming your mission will guide not only what we've previously discussed but also everything to follow. When you hear the word *"mission,"* you often think of a company's mission statement. Which, by all means, is absolutely real, and every company has one (or should have one). It defines the "why" behind the company — *why the company exists.* But in the context of this chapter and this book, we're going to talk about a personal mission. A very similar concept to the company's mission statement, only this mission statement is what drives *you* as a person to achieve all that it is you desire in life.

A mission statement is an ultimate objective that someone has built their life's purpose around. A purposeful direction that includes smaller objectives, goals, and measurables.

Why is this personal mission statement so important to have? When you know where you're heading, the ride will be a bit smoother and more meaningful. Just like a company mission outlines their overall purpose, your personal mission outlines what a balanced life includes and, more importantly, what it does not include.

Now we know that a mission statement is an overall objective — they tend to be relatively general and not so specific, purposely. A vision statement, on the other hand, is more explicit. Visions are rather how you are going to achieve this overall mission; *what does achieving this mission look like? Where do you aim to be?*

To give you a real-world example, let's look at two mission and vision statements. One set is a company mission and vision statement, and the other set is a personal mission and vision statement.

Tesla, Inc. Mission – Tesla's mission is to accelerate the world's transition to sustainable energy.

Tesla, Inc. Vision – Tesla believes the faster the world stops relying on fossil fuels and moves towards a zero-emission future, the better.

Notice Tesla's mission is pretty general. They don't mention anything about their modern electric cars. They're on a mission to accelerate our world's transition to sustainable energy. Period.

What Tesla envisions is a world that stops relying on fossil fuels and moves toward a zero-emission future (primarily through the widespread adoption of electric cars).

Tesla knows its higher purpose — its mission — and they envision what that kind of outcome looks like and what must be done to achieve it. Now, let's compare personal statements.

Personal Mission – I exist to provide opportunities for learning, growth, and significance in young professionals worldwide.

Personal Vision – I believe that mentoring, founding nonprofit and for-profit companies, and writing self-education books will provide young professionals with core opportunities.

Again, the mission statement is fairly general and doesn't say precisely *how* rather *why* I exist and what I'll accomplish. Then the vision statement tells us *how*; what must be done to achieve the mission. The vision is also seen as the outcome.

Fun fact, these are my mission and vision statements. Let's jump into a couple of examples of how you can develop yours.

SELF ASSESSMENTS

Piece together mission statement, vision, KPI's, SMART Goals, and timelines (Ch. 15 Example D, Example E, and Example F).

"Knowing and focusing on your purpose in life gives you perfect direction in knowing what to say yes and no to. Success in life is not about 'getting caught up' but about knowing your priorities." – Nolen Rollins, Entrepreneur, Pastor, and Chairman

Nolen has founded multiple nonprofit companies, including a church, a city foundation, and a global mentorship program. His life of duty goes well beyond just this, though.

Nolen has obtained such a balance in his life by understanding what his life's mission is and what his life's visions are. When you know where you're going and your purpose, your life sets the course in the right direction. This sense of importance and purpose can drive people to do the impossible and go far beyond the limits they once thought they faced. Nolen also mentioned the importance of priorities — we'll get into that in a couple more chapters.

Growing up, I was very fortunate to have identified a higher purpose in myself. I've always confidently known I was placed on this Earth for a more significant reason than just to live and have fun. It was a voice inside, but far more elaborate than just *"I'm going to do great things."* Everyone is going to do great things. But what is your great thing? What is your higher purpose? Why are you here, *alive*?

As I got older, my mission and vision became more explicit, and I knew I had to make an impact on lives across the world. Millions of lives. I feel I've been blessed and am being used by the Universe to live not just for myself but for everyone around me.

I knew from an early age, and I think we all do. But some of us choose to ignore that voice or feel it's not good enough. Trust me when I say listen to that voice; apply your mission to everyday life, and you will see the reflection occur overtime. Your vision will be laid out in front of you, and you will be unstoppable.

Another trick that I've applied to my awareness of mission and vision is to observe prosperous and significant people who do good for the world, and in my way, model their styles of behavior. I'm not saying be the next Joaquin Phoenix or Will Smith, but modeling their actions can be a guide to putting the right energy in the right places.

Never compare yourself to someone else, you'd be doing yourself a disservice. With all due respect to everyone, we are each meant to be whole. You're the first and only *you*. I'm the first and only *me*.

"If I told you how confident I was for the future, you wouldn't believe me. But your belief is not needed." – Conor 'The Notorious' McGregor, Professional Mixed Martial Artist and Entrepreneur

Let's touch on the timeframes; the concept of long term versus short term missions. First and foremost, I suggest having both. The short term tends to be three to five years while long term being 10+ years to a lifetime. Again, these are your missions. Vision will be specific to each of those once the purpose is determined.

Vision statements heavily relate to your objectives and goals. As we've discussed, the vision clarifies how you'll achieve that mission and what the achievement will include — what it looks like.

Tesla's electric car vision to its global sustainability mission. My mentorship and entrepreneurialism vision to my global educational and growth mission.

But now, how do we even achieve these visions? This is where your objectives and goals step in.

In the next chapter, we're taking a deep dive into all of this, so stay with me. The critical thing to understand right here and now is that the more structure you provide yourself, the more effective you will be.

"Chase the vision, not the money; the money will end up following you." – Tony Hsieh, Tech Entrepreneur and Venture Capitalist

Spirituality.

Let's just open up the idea of applying your mission to religion and vice versa — your religion to the mission. In more recent years, my spiritual beliefs have positively impacted my ability to recognize my purpose and lock down my mission. When I take the time to pray, attend Church, and read religious literature, I always find myself in higher thought and self-awareness. I feel a more reliable connection, and it's as if stepping stones are laid in front of me — often when I need them most.

Religion has given me confidence in those voices that I'd heard growing up. It has shed light on my higher purpose, and for it, I feel eternally grateful.

I encourage any of my readers to bridge your religion with your mission, whatever that religion may be. I support you, I endorse your belief, and I support the idea that we are all here for a reason. Find your purpose through progressive thinking and apply it through a mission and vision.

I participated in the fall 2019 Y Combinator Startup School, where I came across a startup similar to Fieldr. The Philadelphia-based company, Dream2Career (D2C), works with businesses, schools, workforce, and community groups to promote and manage events and learning experiences at one-fifth the cost of other media solutions. Their founder and CEO, Kathleen Houlihan, Ph.D., was willing to provide a statement for this specific chapter. I asked Kathleen, "*How does one's Mission and Vision relate to their ability to balance life and everything in it?*" Her response:

"The best way to create a balance between life and a personal mission is to make sure work satisfies that mission. The true issue, the very heart of the problem, is that there is a breakdown in society. Most parents don't have a mission and go through life 'just trying to get by.' This notion negatively impacts their children and society. According to the CDC, youth suicide rates increased by 56% in the last decade (https://www.wsj.com/articles/youth-suicide-rate-rises-56-in-decade-cdc-says-11571284861). The APA (American Psychological Association) points to a correlation between job satisfaction and an individual's mental wellbeing (https://www.apa.org/monitor/2019/03/trends-suicide). Therefore, it is critical that students and young people are given the opportunity to dream and to be inspired through learning experiences that help them to form a personal mission. Work-learn connections help students to network and to see opportunities beyond their environment. As the mission is established through relationships and experiences, individuals find hope for a better future. The development of a personal mission is the only way an individual can experi-

ence a balanced, happy life." – Kathleen Houlihan, Ph.D., Entrepreneur and Public Speaker

Know the direction, and you will know what needs to be balanced. Your questions will be answered, your doubt diminished.

When you've got that mission and vision statement written down on a whiteboard or maybe a notepad, look at it every day. Remind yourself *who* you are and *why* you're here. Then go about your day balancing everything that gets thrown your way, like a boss.

WRITE SOME NOTES

Use this section to write down some thoughts about what your mission and vision statement might be. If you already have them, write them anyway as a refresher. It's always great to *see* what you're *thinking*, as a constant reminder for why it is you're here. A great mission starts with, "I exist to …"

____

____

____

____

____

____

____

____

____

____

____

____

____

____

____

____

____

Having a mission and vision relates to goal setting and achieving. Notice the *achieving* part. We don't want you just to write this stuff down and then forget or fall short. We want you to accomplish that mission and vision. And the way to do that is through firm goals.

This next chapter will cover a ton of information that I've learned over the years about practical goal setting and structuring.

Let's roll on!

Chapter Six.
Goal Setting and Achieving

"Lesson #1,000 – You need a timeline/deadline, or it will always get pushed to the back burner." – Karl Gibbons, Serial Entrepreneur, Motivational Speaker, Chairman, and Business Consultant

Now, let's get into some nitty-gritty of applying this ability to identify progress. After all, Gary Vaynerchuk always reminds his fans and audience that self-awareness is power.

So how do your mission, vision, and strengths relate to your goals? For starters, it is crucial to identify the five "W's" and one "H." The who, what, when, where, why, and how. The direction.

To set the active and meaningful goals that will take you to the *Promised Land* you seek, you must know the strengths for which to apply. Let's say you've identified them for the sake of this chapter and for not being so repetitive.

First and foremost, you can now set achievable yet challenging goals that will accelerate your success. Setting goals can be viewed in various ways, even termed as "objectives" sometimes. But either way, goals are, in fact, objectives that you're pursuing to achieve for the benefit of progression in your life.

Some people set goals to lose weight, some to make more money, others to build relationships. But we all share unique goals that ultimately will define our vision. I prefer to set multiple levels of goals.

Sustainable Development Goals for business purposes, Personal Health and Wellness Goals to focus on just that, Quarterly Advancements (I'll explain this in a bit), and some more goals span a variety of endeavors in my life. Organized much? You bet — all the best leaders are organized. Each and every goal that I set is measurable as well. This is truly where "objective" and "goal" differentiate from one another.

Objectives will be broader. For instance, publishing a book, starting a company, and educating students are all objectives — very broad ones. Now goals, on the other hand, are measurable. There is a proven method called *"SMART Goals"* to abide by.

Specific, Measurable, Attainable, Realistic, Timely.

Notice the elaborative difference between objectives and goals. You want to set both for yourself. Typically, I'll set quarterly Objects and Key Results (OKRs), or in other words, specific goals for each objective. For instance, self-publishing a book about life balance to be available on Amazon by mid-2020. Now that's a goal — and aligns with the five-letter acronym read as *"SMART."* Or even, launching an ed-tech platform for high school students by the start of the fall 2020 school term. Another one, join a gym with a buddy and lose 25lbs by the end of the year.

Set SMART Goals. Smash and repeat.

You can thank me later when you see leaps and bounds made on a monthly, or even sometimes weekly, basis when you get into the groove of setting and attaining goals.

On a further note, make them a bit challenging, similar to the ones you just read. Nothing like "read a few chapters of a book by the end of the month." I mean, c'mon, you should read a few chapters in one or maybe two sittings. You should have the book *finished* by the end of the month; now, that's a bit more challenging for those who have very packed productive schedules.

HOW TO USE SMART

I was doing some deep diving into SMART Goals and fortunately came across this thorough breakdown on Mind Tools' website. Author and businessman, Paul J. Meyer, is the founder of Success Motivation International and describes the characteristics of SMART goals in his 2003 book, "*Attitude Is Everything: If You Want to Succeed Above and Beyond.*" The Mind Tools content team did a phenomenal job of elaborating on what these goals imply, so why try and reinvent the wheel, right? Let's dive into Mind Tool's report:

"1. Specific – Your goal should be clear and specific, otherwise you won't be able to focus your efforts or feel truly motivated to achieve it. When drafting your goal, try to answer the five 'W' questions:

What do I want to accomplish? Why is this goal important? Who is involved? Where is it located?

Example – Imagine that you are currently a marketing executive, and you'd like to become head of marketing. A specific goal could be, 'I want to gain the skills and experience necessary to become head of marketing within my organization so that I can build my career and lead a successful team.'

2. Measurable – It's important to have measurable goals so that you can track your progress and stay motivated. Assessing progress helps you to stay focused, meet your deadlines, and feel the excitement of getting closer to achieving your goal. A measurable goal should address questions such as:

How much? How many? How will I know when it is accomplished?

Example – You might measure your goal of acquiring the skills to become head of marketing by determining that you will have completed the necessary training courses and gained the relevant experience within five years' time.

3. Attainable – Your goal also needs to be realistic and attainable to be successful. In other words, it should stretch your abilities but still remain possible.

When you set an achievable goal, you may be able to identify previously overlooked opportunities or resources that can bring you closer to it. An attainable goal will usually answer questions such as:

How can I accomplish this goal? How realistic is the goal, based on other constraints, such as financial factors?

Example – You might need to ask yourself whether developing the skills required to become head of marketing is realistic, based on your existing experience and qualifications. For example, do you have the time to complete the required training effectively? Are the necessary resources available to you? Can you afford to do it?

Tip: Beware setting goals that someone else has power over. For example, 'Get that promotion!' depends on who else applies, and on the recruiter's decision. But 'Get the experience and training that I need to be considered for that promotion' is entirely down to you.

4. Realistic – This step is about ensuring that your goal matters to you and that it also aligns with other relevant goals. We all need support and assistance in achieving our goals, but it's important to retain control over them. So, make sure that your plans drive everyone forward, but that you're still responsible for achiev-

ing your own goal. A relevant goal can answer 'yes' to these questions:

Does this seem worthwhile? Is this the right time? Does this match our other efforts/needs? Am I the right person to reach this goal?

Example – You might want to gain the skills to become head of marketing within your organization, but is it the right time to undertake the required training, or work toward additional qualifications? Are you sure that you're the right person for the head of a marketing role? Have you considered your spouse's goals? For example, if you want to start a family, would completing training in your free time make this more difficult?

5. Timely – Every goal needs a target date so that you have a deadline to focus on and something to work toward. This part of the SMART goal criteria helps to prevent everyday tasks from taking priority over your longer-term goals. A time-bound goal will usually answer these questions:

When? What can I do six months from now? What can I do six weeks from now? What can I do today?

Example – Gaining the skills to become head of marketing may require additional training or experience, as we mentioned earlier. How long will it take you to acquire these skills? Do you need further training, so that you're eligible for certain exams or qualifications? It's important to give yourself a realistic time frame for accomplishing the smaller goals that are necessary to achieving your final objective."

Serial entrepreneur Karl Gibbons and I had the pleasure of connecting over this book, and he was kind enough to share a response to a critical question that I had for him. I asked, *"How do setting goals relate to one's ability to balance life and everything in it?"* Karl's response falls perfectly in line with SMART goals.

"Think, set, and use your business goals like the GPS in your car. Decide where you want to go, set the route, and use the system to help you highlight gas stations, road works, and any other specific areas or points of interest during the journey. Based on this data, you can decide which route to take.

When it comes to goal setting, many entrepreneurs start with good intentions, and by the end of the day, it's all gone to hell in a handbasket. Just take the beginning of the year, for example, how many people on New Year's Eve make a resolution that they're going to the gym, they're going to lose some weight, they're going to get fit this year. Off they run to the gym, buy an annual membership and by the third week in January, for 75 to 80 percent of them, that's it, they're done. The first thing is *that they don't follow through. The next thing is they try to eat the elephant — (tackle the problem) — in one bite. They've set goals that are too high and lofty; what they need to do is break those goals down. If you were to think in terms of a 90-day cycle, for example, that's smart, because it's a small chunk of time, very measurable, very achievable, and you can measure your successes over those 90 days. What people usually do is decide they're going to turn the business around, but they're just not being specific. When someone says they've got to increase sales, that's not a goal, that's just a statement, but if you say you've got to increase sales from a million to $1.5M, then that's specific, and it's measurable. If you don't set specific goals, they're not measurable, and they may be unachievable. Therefore they're not realistic, and you're not giving yourself the time in which to attain them.*

What I've just spelled out is the acronym' SMART,' Specific, Measurable, Achievable, Realistic, and within a Timescale. Make that every 90 days. It'll work. It will become a habit or what a sportsperson calls muscle memory — you just get into a positive and productive routine. It works.” – Karl Gibbons, Serial Entrepreneur, Motivational Speaker, Chairman, and Business Consultant

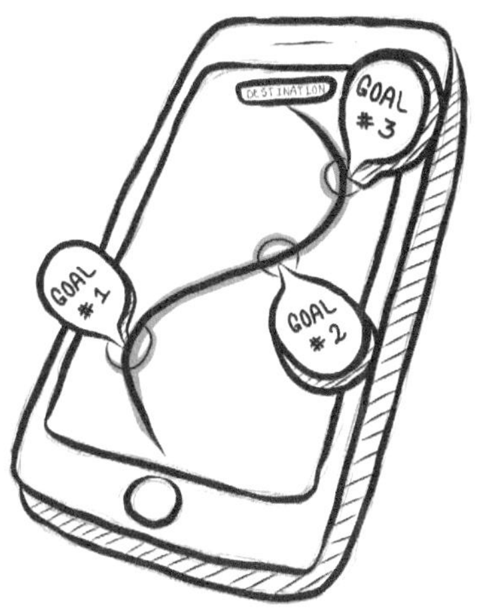

Always, and I mean always have goals — pebbles to rocks to mountains. It's essential to have goals in mind at all times, so you're making conscious decisions daily. Decisions that will produce results — decisions that will allow you to attain those goals.

Smash goals then rise out of the comfort zone.

Fun fact, the comfort zone is where hopes and dreams go to die. What I mean by this is while you're sitting in the comfort zone of life, you're hindering your ability to grow as an individual. All of those hopes and dreams that you have will wither away in the overbearing ease that the comfort zone is. It's easy; it's unchallenging; it's unprogressive. Don't let your hopes and dreams die in the comfort zone.

I mentioned in this chapter that I like to have multiple sets of these objectives and goals. If you're someone who's got a few different endeavors going on, it might be wise to lock those objectives and goals down in each one. The more strategic and smarter you work, the more effective your results will be.

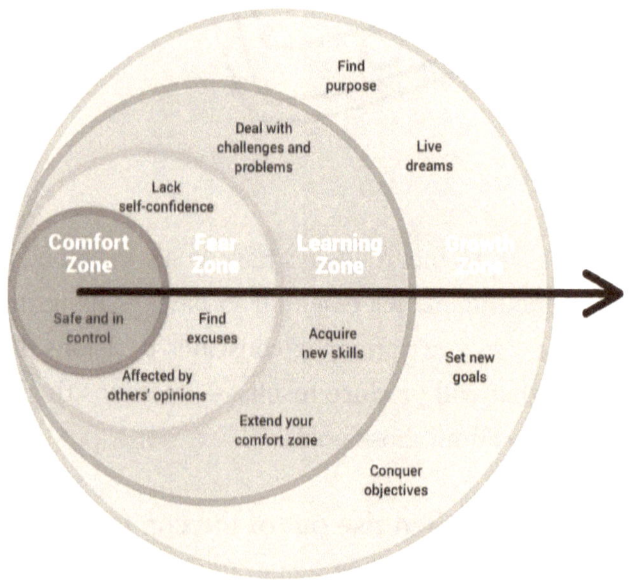

(https://medium.com/@hassan.naeem101/how-i-plan-to-become-a-better-learner-5cba9e9ed04c)

"The way to get started is to quit talking and begin doing." – Walt Disney, Entrepreneur, Animator, Voice Actor, and Film Producer

SELF ASSESSMENTS

Quarterly Assessments; 90 Day Start, Stop, Increase, Decrease (Credit to Karl Gibbons) (Ch. 15 Example A).

"Living life without goals is like going through the world with a blindfold on." – Jakub Adamowicz, Tech Entrepreneur and Real Estate Agent

As a tech startup founder and CEO, Jakub knows what it's like to have his life always being in constant, ever-evolving balance. And to achieve such balance for the sake of himself, his company, his family, staff, etc., he knows that setting goals is a priority.

Without these goals, you're simply strolling through life with a blindfold on, missing opportunities left and right. Opportunities that would heavily relate to those strengths we hope you've identified. If you can't see your life for what it is and could be, how on Earth are you going to balance it?

Breakdown and analyze your goals.

Do they apply to your mission? This ties into the concept of having a thorough set of SMART Goals and even objectives for those goals. Once identified and written down on a spreadsheet — or however you record most effectively — break them down and analyze them. Do they have anything to do with what you're here on this planet to accomplish? Or are they arbitrary goals that you want to achieve for the wrong reasons, such as just having your name on something?

Analyze these goals to ensure that what you're about to commit your valuable time and effort to, will provide a progression in your life. Ensure they are going to continuously lay the path down for where you genuinely want to go.

Know where you're heading and ensure goals apply to growth. Having the vision of what you want your life to be like is going to define those goals. Let's repeat that. Your goals should not identify what your vision is; your vision should determine what your goals are going to be. This breakdown of goals will shed light on whether or not they apply to the growth of oneself.

There's nothing wrong with figuring it out as you go, as you should. But wouldn't it be nice to have a few mental road signs (not blocks) to lead you to your milestones throughout life? Notice how I said "through life," not "through the motions." Never just go through the motions.

Like we've discussed, always be a student and always be open to learning; always be open-minded and continue figuring "it" out as you go. Can I give you a hint, though? There's no such thing as figuring "it" out. *It* doesn't exist. And it's not supposed to. There is no "it."

So enjoy the journey, appreciate it, and you will have an endless amount of destinations.

Only they won't be final destinations — just another stop on your journey through life. So, wouldn't it make sense to have a few mental road signs along the way to lead you to those destinations, those milestones? It sure would. That's what compelling visions, objectives, and goals will provide.

Be selective in your goal setting.

Don't chase too many rabbits; you won't ever catch one. When he originated this concept, what Confucius was referring to is that if you're trying to chase multiple rabbits all at once, you're never going to catch even one of them.

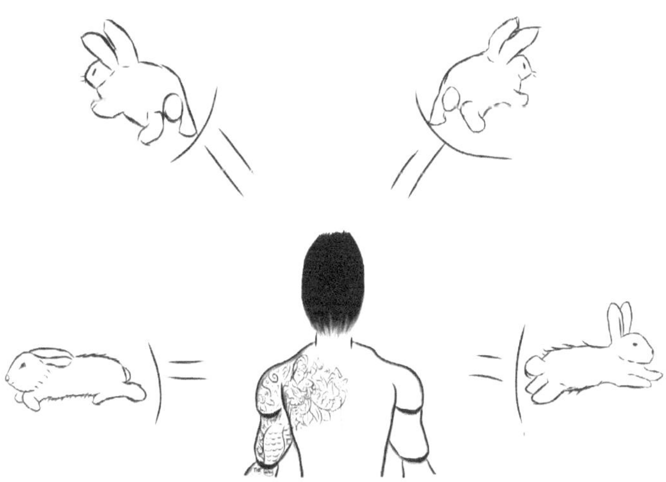

If you're trying to do three different things at one time, it will deplete your quality of work and the ability to achieve even one of them. Of course, scalability does apply. And by that, I mean if you're trying to cook while texting while watching Netflix, then that's what most Gen Z'ers do daily anyway. If you're attempting to launch a nonprofit, work full time, and raise a family, that's going to get very tough.

Once you've filled up your plate with a variety of tasks and work needed, you risk overloading your ability to balance it all. It's challenging to allocate the proper amount of time and brainpower that each endeavor requires, and to each one consistently.

Maybe continue working full time while raising your family, and once you're in a fiscal position to quit that job, then take the nonprofit idea head-on. It will get the proper amount of attention and resources it needs to get off the ground, and then sooner than later turn income to you.

For those who didn't know, yes, you absolutely can pay yourself while running a nonprofit. In fact, you still need to drive sufficient numbers for sustainability purposes; the allocation of funds are just treated differently than a for-profit business.

Measure your balance and ability to retain it by goal-setting (and smashing). Remember how we set SMART Goals? Well, these are the goals that are measured and can be tangible in the balance of life. They're the pebbles in the scale, to pinpoint where that balance is.

Set your goals, collect your pebbles, and balance life. And don't just reach those goals, smash them.

WRITE SOME NOTES

Let's write down some goals! And by us, I mean *you*! Take a minute or two to review some current goals that you have. Are they SMART Goals? Are they challenging enough as to where you'll see the progression in your life? Maybe set yourself one objective for the next few months and three core SMART Goals to achieve under that objective.

Take it away.

"An idiot with a plan can beat a genius without a plan." – Warren Buffet, Business Magnate, Investor, and Philanthropist

Goal setting relates to prioritization. By now, you probably have a handful of strategic goals in your mind or on paper. But where do you start?

The *prioritization*, as we'll discuss here momentarily, of your goals is a keynote for strategizing how you're going to smash them or when you're going to start. This next chapter will define what prioritizing your life and goals means.

Chapter Seven.
Prioritization of What's "On Your Plate"

Okay, so you've identified your strengths, and you've identified your goals. Now you've got a full plate of tasks, responsibilities, deadlines to meet, and expectations to fulfill. You must break down goals and know the steps.

If you don't have a thorough understanding of what it is you're chasing, it's going to be challenging to identify where to begin. This is why prioritization is such an imperative role in the effectiveness of smashing those goals.

This chapter will help you better understand what it is on that plate that needs immediate attention and how much attention.

First, let's define prioritization — it's pretty simple. Priorities are the most important, usually, most urgent things in your life. Prioritization is just the act of deciding what the priorities are. It's ... wait for it ... strategy! It's working smart and not just hard.

Keep what's most important at the top.

As you begin deciding what is most important — what you should start pursuing or which goals to start smashing — it is critical to keep in mind that the higher the priority, the higher on the list it needs to be. And by higher on the list, I mean of the first or *the* very first goal(s) that you tackle.

Setting the priorities ahead of not-as-important or pressing goals will put you in a very productive setting. You'll have clarity on what you need to begin working on right away and what you need to get done to progress effectively.

Jeff Bezos always advocates for doing the most important things first in your day, as early as you can. This will kickstart your day, offer a tremendous sense of relief and accomplishment, and will put you in a position for daily growth.

Once you've started and completed those initial priorities, work towards the bottom of the listed goals or tasks. Most often, the less of a priority it is, the easier and simpler it's going to be to achieve that goal.

The priorities are *highly* valuable — high risk/high reward — and those are the hurdles you're leaping over. The lower priorities on your list of to-dos are going to be your skips to the finish line.

Applying physical and mental activity before that problematic task will make all the world's difference — workout/meditate/journal thoughts. I've always noticed when I'm able to get a workout in or just meditate before starting my list of goals or to-dos, my performance is through the roof.

This ties right into the science of taking on the most important things first, and early on in the day. Your brain is highly stimulated, mind and body are in sync, and the clarity of thought will allow you to focus so keenly on what you're doing post-workout.

Wake up and start the day with a walk, maybe a workout, or perhaps find a quiet space in the house and meditate for 10 to 15 minutes. Then smash those priorities.

SELF ASSESSMENTS

**Schedule Analysis (Ch. 15 Example C).
12 to 15 Things to say "NO" to (Ch. 15 Example
D). List and Strikethrough. Assess Quarterly.**

"It is not enough to be busy. So are the ants. The question is, 'What are we busy with?'" – Henry David Thoreau, Essayist, Poet, and Philosopher

I mentioned earlier in this book that I've traded the word *"busy"* for *"productive."* Well, this quote certainly sums up my motive for doing so. This simple concept tests the progress that one is making, or thinks they are making.

Ants are busy.

It's one thing to be busy, but it's a whole other thing to be productive. When you're productive, you're prioritizing. When you're productive, you're smashing goals that are moving you forward every step of the way. The strategy to begin your work is so in-tune that nothing could throw you off course. Be productive by prioritizing; don't just be busy.

I encourage my readers to do the same as I have done. Substitute "busy" with "productive" when you're talking to people — I can assure you they'll notice it and be impressed. You'll gain credibility now that you're "productive" daily. Your colleagues will look up to you; you'll become a leader when you're always productive and not just busy. And most importantly, you'll encrypt a message into your subconscious to move through life with constant prioritization and a real sense of accomplishment.

Remember, it all begins with you internally — set the right tone for your day-to-day and watch life unfold at a progressive pace.

Time management is vital to this matter.

We've talked about placing the higher priorities on the top of the list; they come first and they come early. Well, time management plays a significant role in the success of this ability. If your schedule is all over the place, nothing is set in stone, and you can't find the time for these priorities, then you're not going to see any sort of progress — at least nothing valuable. Work on that time management, and you'll find strength in prioritization.

A massive factor in managing time is the ability to say *"no"* more often than not. Saying "no" to going out when you have work to finish. Saying "no" to taking on a new project or endeavor when your plate is already full. Saying "no" to vacation when you have a significant responsibility right around the corner in which you need to prepare for. We are asked to do many things throughout every day, and the willpower to say "no" more often than not will allow you to effectively manage the limited amount of time you have.

Reference the self-assessment tools that have been recommended to you earlier in this chapter, to begin breaking down *what* it is that you must manage and the appropriate *amount of time* needed for each.

No TV.

Here's a little tip that I can *guarantee* will result in more time for you to manage priorities: stop with the hours upon hours of Netflix. Seriously. Without a single drop of doubt in my body, I know that one of the biggest reasons I'm able to manage time tremendously well is because I ruled out TV shows from my life a long time ago. And I'm not kidding one bit — I don't watch TV shows.

Movies, on the other hand, I can enjoy during an evening after I've finished everything for the day, and I'm even ahead of schedule for the days to come.

But TV shows I find to be a waste of precious time. The time that I need to be prioritizing and managing critical things in life. The time that it's going to take to build the life that I want, instead of just entertaining myself by watching other people live it on TV.

So, I implore you — no, I dare you — to reduce Netflix and other streaming services to a minimum, especially the TV shows. Why do I keep specifying TV shows? Because they are an unnecessary commitment. You commit yourself to one episode after the next because you *"must find out what happens next,"* and because you *"must watch the following season."* Countless hours, gone — hours you'll never get back.

Movies, on the other hand, you watch one and get the entire plot; there is no urge to keep watching more to find out what happens next; no season after season, stealing your limited amount of time.

So again, I dare you just to reduce the TV shows — or flat out remove them from your life like I have — and watch as you become 10x more productive and can accomplish something in a few months that would take a binge-watcher a year.

Build a routine schedule once consistent.

This removes the need for too many unnecessary decisions. Now let's say you've been doing your best to remain consistent in your schedule. You've found the groove of when breakfast, lunch, and dinner need to be, when meetings should usually be scheduled, when you're going to get your exercise, family time, etc. Make this schedule a routine, so you're able to adequately prepare before each day; you're ready to think into the future and have a strong sense of what you might be doing and when.

All of this will not only influence prioritizing goals but also will decrease the likelihood of decision fatigue. With a routine schedule, much of what you'll be doing does not require substantial decisions. You know you've got to be at the gym by 7am, so get yourself there; there's no *deciding* to do. You know that afternoons are blocked off for a meeting and phone calls; there's no reason to take on a new project that would require afternoon attention.

Once you've found a schedule that fits your liking and lifestyle, make it habitual, and you'll allow for effective prioritization and decision-making.

Before you're like *"well, that's just not possible,"* I'm not saying that once your schedule is routine, it's as if nothing can be adjusted. Not at all. Undoubtedly, be flexible, but with a conscious mind, you may be taking away valuable time dedicated to a priority.

Simplify the fundamentals by making them a habit; make them a lifestyle. Let's briefly tie in Chapter Three

— *Life's Fundamentals.* Just like you build out your schedule for your day-to-day, to-dos, and priorities, I highly encourage making your life easier by treating fundamentals as such.

Set time aside at night — you need to shut it all off and get proper *sleep*, in addition to the time you need to get up in the morning and prepare for a great day. In other words, have a strict bedtime and alarm clock!

Same with *nutrition*. Know when you're able to eat breakfast, eat lunch, and eat dinner all while drinking plenty of water. Build those into your routine.

And last, but by no means least, *love*. Set aside the family time with the spouse and kiddos, set aside time for yourself to wind down, and do some reading.

Again, build it into the schedule. Make this all a habit, and soon you will have a lifestyle that you have full control of. How? Because you curated this lifestyle to align with stable fundamentals, practical priorities, and goals that will take you places much farther than you can even believe.

I got the chance to talk with a good friend of mine and colleague — better known in the community as the RoomDig Founder and CEO — Jakub Adamowicz. Jakub is continuously balancing a variety of tasks on his plate, as mentioned earlier in this book, between his staff, wife, friends, and much more. With a lot on his plate at all times, Jakub needs to have a strong sense of prioritization to ensure the efforts he's putting in daily are going to the right places. When I asked Jakub, *"How does Prioritization of what's 'on your plate' relate to one's ability to balance life and everything in it?"* He had this to say:

"Prioritization is crucial because it makes sure time is being spent most effectively. It comes down to what progress and happiness mean for an individual, but for the most part, if you aren't prioritizing things that bring you happiness and put you ahead, then you're going the opposite direction." – Jakub Adamowicz, Tech Entrepreneur and Real Estate Agent

It takes effort to achieve intricate and challenging things, but you also see the most return on your "investments." The most important of priority goals will often be challenging — *always* if I'm honest. And I would hope so — remember these goals should be challenging because that's where the most growth will reside.

Money is not always the investment made into these goals, these priorities. Instead, it is your highly valuable time and what you're willing to sacrifice to focus on achieving these goals. If you put in the time and effort to start that company, the return on your investment will provide invaluable knowledge, experience, and hopefully, lots of money as well. The investment of your time on a Friday afternoon to build that home playground for your kids will provide you a return of smiles, laughter, and a lifetime of memories. The investment of your time and efforts into working with a local nonprofit will give you the return of pride, wisdom, self-awareness, and good karma.

The better you can prioritize, the larger and faster you'll see that progress. The most progress is made in challenging times; times, you're pulled out of your comfort zone and must push your abilities' limits. This is when you discover new talents within new ideas, new perspectives, and overall growth in life. Every challenge is different for all of us, but we share the commonality of developing ourselves into a better version than we were when it was easy.

"Without commitment, you'll never start. But more importantly, without consistency, you'll never finish. It's not easy. If it were easy, there'd be no Carry Washington...If it were easy, there'd be no Denzel Washington. So, keep working, keep striving. Never give up. Fall down seven times, stand up eight. Ease is a greater threat to progress than hardship. So keep moving, keep growing, keep learning. See you at work." – Denzel Washington, Actor, Movie Director, and Producer

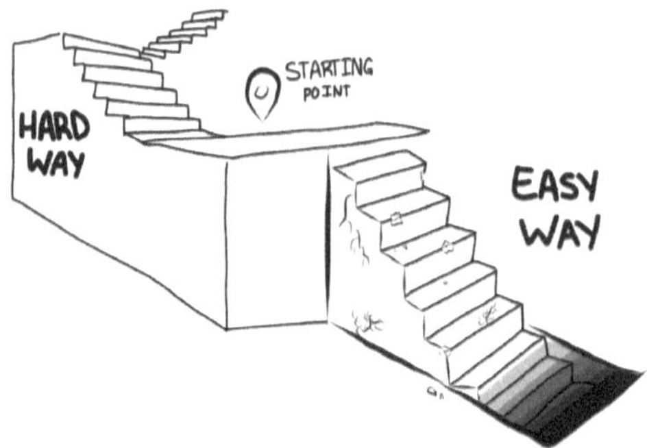

Prioritize, ladies and gentlemen. It will not be easy. It will be challenging. But this is where your growth and success resides.

Remain consistent in your approach. Watch for patterns and failures — patterns *of* failure. Learn from these and apply them to your prioritization of tasks.

Lockdown that path and remain consistent. Progress will come. It's not just about how you start, but if and how you follow through to the finish line — just as Denzel put it. Given balance is always changing and molding, having the ability to prioritize will allow for consistent growth and progress through difficult times.

WRITE SOME NOTES

Take this moment now to refine some of those goals you wrote down in the previous chapter. Flip back to the page if you need to. Refine these and markdown which ones are priorities. Are you working on those already? Have you been putting them off because they're more challenging? Be honest with yourself and make today the day you start focusing on the priorities in your life.

Prioritization relates to the delegation. Now that you've got your list of priorities and other goals, and you've identified strengths and weaknesses, in walks "delegation."

Are you getting a sense of sequential chapters yet? Each of these chapters has transitioned into the next one strategically, as each applies to one another.

Without goals, you don't know your priorities, and without priorities, you won't know what to delegate. This next chapter will elaborate on assigning tasks, to-dos, and weaknesses to others with the reason of working smart and not just hard.

Chapter Eight.
The Beauty of Delegation

"Most people don't get those experiences because they never ask. I've never found anybody that didn't want to help me if I asked them for help." – Steve Jobs, Business Magnate, Industrial Designer, Investor, and Media Proprietor

Know your strengths and priorities, and delegate weaknesses to a team for help. We're bundling a few chapters together here with this single chapter on delegation. But let's start by defining the word, so we're all on the same page (no pun intended).

By definition, *to delegate* means to *"assign responsibility or authority."* Now usually, it is used in the context of the workplace — a boss assigning a project to the Marketing Director, Susan, or the whole marketing department. Maybe Susan delegated the analytical reports to Tom because she's too focused on her strength, which is the project's branding. Let's continue to use this example.

Great leaders can prioritize tasks and delegate other tasks to a team. Susan has been able to break down the project objectives and goals. She understands the team's roles, and more importantly, their skills. She prioritizes the critical to-dos as the first to-dos, and she does this for each segment of the project.

Let's say these segments are branding, analytics, and partnerships. As a great leader, Susan is going to delegate these goals and responsibilities to the *right* people within each segment. This method of enabling leverages the strengths of Susan's team but also their weaknesses.

Susan knows she's not skilled at analytics, so that's going to Tom. She knows it's going to Tom because he's a bit introverted and loves his numbers, so he might not be the best to handle partnerships. And because this is a well-oiled team, Karen, our third team member, is managing the partnerships. Why? Because Karen loves to talk and is already comfortable asking for the manager.

Susan, Tom, and Karen all have their strengths and their weaknesses. As a leader, Susan was able to delegate the roles and responsibilities of the project to the *right* people to get the job done.

I'm very thankful to be sitting on the first-ever Legacy Leadership Forum based in Estero, Florida. Our Founder and President, Nolen Rollins, gave a keynote on effective leadership during our March 2020 meet-up. Fortunately, Nolen has permitted me to include his presentation content right in this book. Gold, right!? Absolute gold.

Below are seven keynotes that Nolen stands by when teaching and instilling leadership. And not just Nolen, but also a gentleman by the name of Peter Drucker. Yes, Peter Drucker, the "management consultant, educator, and author, whose writings contributed to the philosophical and practical foundations of the modern business corporation." Nolen and Peter were involved in the same finely knit network of mentorship; Nolen's mentor was Peter's mentee.

The keynotes are as follows:

1. Enlist the Right People on Your Team.
    a. Constantly be looking for sharp individuals.

    b. Know the kind of people you want on your team.

    c. Enlist based more on desired characteristics rather than desired skills.

    d. Enlist individuals to build a balanced team.

    e. Have a designed enlistment process.

        i. Candidate File

        ii. Resumes

        iii. Applications

        iv. Assessments

        v. Interview Process

    f. Develop a corporate culture of "recognition" of great leaders.

2. Examine the Strengths and Weaknesses of All Team Members.

    a. Know each team member's Personal Profile:

        i. Personality

        ii. Experiences

        iii. Abilities

        iv. Strengths

        v. Passions

        vi. Spiritual Gifts

        vii. Core Values

    b. Recommended Assessment Resources:

        i. DISC Personality Assessment

        ii. StrengthFinders 2.0

iii. GPS Team Workshop

c. Develop a corporate culture of "understanding" of all team members.

3. Engage Each Team Member in the Right Position/ Responsibilities.

a. Success in getting people in the right job is based on knowing your team.

b. Allow people to work out of their strengths.

c. Enlist, delegate, complement each other's weaknesses.

d. Periodically evaluate and reassign responsibilities.

e. Allow job description to align with strengths and successful performance.

f. Develop a corporate culture of "team" where everyone is better together.

4. Equip Each Team Member for Effective Service.

a. Know what each team member needs to be able to be effective.

b. Ask each team member, "What do you need to know (information, skills, etc.) to be even more effective at your job?"

c. Provide information, skills, and training needed for each team member.

d. An important part of equipping (and empowering and encouraging) team members in both formal and informal meetings to keep everyone informed.

e. Develop a corporate culture of "preparation" for effective service.

5. Empower Each Team Member for Success.

a. Train people to take responsibility/ownership of problems, needs, and solutions.

b. Ask each team member, "What do you need (resources, funds, equipment, etc.) to be successful at your job?"

c. Give team members both responsibility and authority within clearly defined boundaries.

d. Make sure team members have access to others they may need to be successful.

e. Develop a corporate culture of "ownership" of successful execution.

6. Encourage Each Team Member Regularly

a. The number one reason people enjoy their work is appreciated by those around them.

b. Recognize that every team member has value and should feel valued.

c. Be a champion of each team member's strengths.

    d. Think, speak, and act as a team – not as individuals.

    e. Genuinely care about every team member.

    f. Simple practical tools for encouragement:

        i. Use of names

        ii. Special recognitions

        iii. Life events

        iv. Asking questions, opinions, and input

    g. Develop a corporate culture of "value" where each team member feels valued.

7. Expect Each Team Member to Give/Do His/Her Best.

    a. Have clearly defined performance expectations.

    b. Reward excellent performance.

    c. Challenge individuals to improve where needed.

    d. Have periodic personal and team goals.

    e. Learn how to deal with individuals who are not giving their best.

    f. Remove individuals who consistently do not meet expectations.

    g. Develop a corporate culture of "honesty and transparency" where team members can express themselves.

This breakdown creates a practical sense of delegation and balance, but it also creates an effective leader if practiced. These seven keynotes and sub-notes have been proven in high-stake environments by highly effective leaders.

Nolen was also kind to share some insightful quotes taken out of the renowned *"Good to Great"* by Jim Collins — another highly recommended book. The following quotes tie vision into the beauty of delegation, especially the importance of it.

"Great vision without great people is irrelevant." – Jim Collins, Researcher, Author, Speaker, and Consultant

"People before vision. People before strategy. People before structure. People before technology." – Jim Collins, Researcher, Author, Speaker, and Consultant

This all applies to our personal goals and priorities as well, but first, another business approach.

Solo founders are rare. Many successful companies are co-founded. Read and reference *"Entrepreneurial Leap"* by Gino Wickman for some fresh content about solo founders versus cofounders or to get a grip on whether or not you've got what it takes to be an entrepreneur. It thoroughly breaks down the data behind there being more cofounders than solo founders, and what you should be looking for in a cofounder if and when you're in a position to delegate responsibility beyond yourself. It's tough to be a lone wolf. Some prefer it and just can't work with a team, but this book will explain why you will need a team sooner than you might think despite being a solo founder.

I've enjoyed launching three startups with some great business partners and friends of mine. This book is my first solo venture. But even then, I've delegated editing, proofreading, graphic design, and even some of the content in this very book!

Everyone has their weaknesses. We've covered this heavily, but let's just reiterate the importance of its relevance to the delegation.

Just like Susan identified her staff's weaknesses as well as her own, we all must know our weaknesses and delegate to-dos and goals to teams. Let's give a more individualistic example.

You're living with your family or have a roommate. You're great at and love landscaping. The elaborative design ability you have is just so natural. You also know how to work all of the equipment properly and safely. You're cool with getting down and dirty. But, the last time you tried cooking dinner, the fire alarm went off, and you destroyed your oven for God knows what reason.

Who do you think should be given the responsibility of cooking Thanksgiving dinner? Not you. Who should be given the responsibility of ensuring the property is looking appealing for guests, though? You guessed it. You are.

That's a simple way of domesticating the concept of delegation through the identification of weakness and strength.

It is a fact that well-rounded people and leaders have their weaknesses and accept them. Once they are understood, you can then effectively delegate to-dos and responsibility altogether to other people in your life.

Just ask.

Trust me; there are people in your life that care and want to see you succeed. It might be a family member, a teacher/professor, a therapist, a friend, or a colleague. Look into your network of people in life, identify their role, and pinpoint who might have a lick of knowledge on what you're struggling with.

And if it ends up being the wrong person, follow up with asking to be pointed in the right direction because that individual or group of people might know where you can receive the help you're looking for.

I know sometimes you might think otherwise, but just remember our earlier chapters about internal emotion and your perspective, as well as surrounding yourself with the right people.

Thou who does not ask, will most often not receive. And those with their mouths closed cannot eat.

Once you identify those weaknesses, you know exactly who you need to hire, who to ask for help from, who to get mentorship from, and more. Don't ever be discouraged from asking for help. Nobody has ever done it entirely alone. Sure, you might hear stories about singers who were an "overnight success." Or an entrepreneur who built a unicorn tech company and sold it overnight (unicorns are privately held startups valued over $1B, often tech companies).

What you don't see is the 10+ years that the singer spent performing at local bars or on street corners, the support from close friends and family to keep going because their "break" was coming, or the vocal coach that trained them since they were eight years old.

How about the *Mark Zucks* of the world? Fun fact, Facebook technically had five cofounders, and Mark had built multiple online platforms before Facebook. *And through Facebook's growth came thousands of more* employees that made it into the big tech behemoth that it is today.

Nobody ever did it alone. Relax, you've got a whole world of supporters. Lose the ego and get the help; build the team. I can promise you that celebrating across the finish line alone is boring.

Once you lose the ego and realize that we're all just figuring *it* out as we go, your mental freedom and independence will be amplified — and the sky becomes the limit.

Legacy Church, Kingdom Mobilization, and Estero Forever Foundation Founder and President, Nolen Rollins, was kind enough further to provide some insight into this topic of delegation. I asked Nolen, *"How does delegation relate to one's ability to balance life and everything in it?"* His response:

"Balancing one's life is all about priorities. I have taught my children and the hundreds of other individuals who have served on teams I have led over the years (over 50) that you should never get 'caught up.'

You will often hear people say, 'I'll do that as soon as I get caught up.' There is always more to do in life for leaders than can ever be done, even by the most efficient time managers in the world. Success in life is not about getting 'caught up.' It is dependent upon your ability and commitment to live by priorities.

Constantly, every day, every moment of every day, you must be conscious of what is the most important thing I should be doing right now. Each individual must focus on the top priorities for that individual. When you do this, that leaves a mountain of other activities that should and must be done by someone else.

Thus, the crucial role of effective delegation. I say 'effective delegation' because successful delegation does not mean you get someone else to do some of the lesser important things on your agenda and hope for the best. Effective delegation is the result of effective team building.

You do not delegate just so you do not have to do something. You delegate because you have helped build a great team, and the team knows what each team member does best.

Effective delegation is dependent upon your ability to enlist great team members, equip these team members with everything they need to be successful, empower them with responsibility and authority, encourage them as they serve well, and expect them to do what they do with excellence.

When this happens, delegation is easy; it is the natural result of leadership and team building. When you delegate to team members who know what to do, how to do it, and the task 'fits' who they are, everyone wins. And you are able to focus on what you do best, live a balanced life, give attention to your top priorities, have a sense of accomplishment and significance, and live happily ever after." – Nolen Rollins, Entrepreneur, Pastor, and Chairman

Team building is a critical ability in balancing.

Great leaders do just that — they lead teams and groups of people by delegating and doing all of the above.

Without the ability to build a team around yourself or a support system, balancing everything on your plate is not going to be just difficult but nearly impossible. And this isn't the type of impossible to try and defy — you would go insane trying to do everything alone.

So get comfortable with building a team, strategically, through your goal setting and prioritization, and you will naturally balance that massive plate of yours. Again, work smarter, not just harder.

Finding the right team can be a process, but the right ones will come across your path naturally when you know what direction to be searching — or even just searching in the first place makes a difference. There's a saying, *"Hard work will put you where luck can find you."* Combine that with *"smart work will put you where help can find you,"* and you've got some gold to live by.

SELF ASSESSMENTS

Identify your weaknesses and pinpoint mentors, family, advisors, teachers, etc., who can help with related tasks (or professional training to strengthen those weaknesses) (Ch. 15 Example B).

"When you delegate work to a member of the team, your job is to clearly frame success and describe the objectives." – Steven Sinofsky, former President of the Windows Division at Microsoft

For this chapter, let's pretend "member of the team" also applies to someone in your life — someone you want to ask for help.

Sinofsky implies that it's our responsibility, as the ones who are doing the delegating, to frame what success of the outcome ought to look like. Pinpoint what the result should be for this goal or to-do. Clearly outlining this will give a sense of direction and the awareness of what real accomplishment will look like once you get to work. The more aware and well-versed your team member is, the more effective the delegation will have been.

Describe the objectives.

We talked a lot about this already. Don't just give the measurable goals, also give overall objectives to your team members for the highest sense of clarity and awareness.

The better the job of elaborating on delegation, the more effective you will be in it. Between you and your team, the balance of work will be stable.

Idolizing the best.

Elon Musk and Peter Thiel co-founded PayPal in 1998, Steve Wozniak and Steve Jobs co-founded Apple in 1976, Mark Zuckerberg and his team co-founded Facebook in 2004, Reed Hastings and Marc Randolph co-founded Netflix in 1997, Melanie Perkins, Cameron Adams, and Cliff Obrecht co-founded Canva in 2012.

The list goes on and on for the best of *the best*. And more often than not, these big-name businessmen and women are where they are now because of the team in whom built the foundation. All of these significant founders had their weaknesses, and they delegated them to the team members who together made what are now multi-million, billion, and trillion-dollar companies.

When trying to do too much and overload your plate, you lose the ability to balance effectively. Instead, it becomes a game of juggling without any proper delegation, and there's not a juggler in this world who hasn't dropped the ball at least once or several times.

But if you do end up in a juggling-like situation, the best thing you can do is identify which balls are *glass* and which are *rubber*. Which will shatter if dropped, and which will bounce right back if dropped. Know the differences, but always try to refrain from juggling in the first place.

WRITE SOME NOTES

We're halfway through the book! If you're still here, I thank you sincerely for the support and commitment.

Now take some of that commitment and use it to write down some thoughts about delegation. Of those priorities that you listed earlier, can any be delegated to a team? Maybe the lesser priorities can be. Perhaps you've got a clear sense of your weaknesses, and it'd be a great moment to align those with a to-do and delegate it. Spill the thoughts.

____

____

____

____

____

____

____

____

____

____

____

____

____

____

____

____

____

____

____

____

____

____

Delegation relates to execution. All right, so we've made some headway with these last chapters.

Between strength finding, mission and vision, goal setting, prioritization, and delegation, you now have a formula for success. Use those chapters sequentially to kick start your progress from point A to B.

But, this is all assuming you're able to follow through. Can you walk the walk? After all, actions speak louder than words. And that is why *execution* is the game, ladies and gentlemen. You can play all you want, but unless you're executing, you're not even *in* the game.

Let's take this next chapter to make sure your head is in the game — to make sure you're going to execute.

"You gotta getcha, getcha, getcha, getcha head in the game." – Troy Bolton, King of East High

Chapter Nine.
Execution is the Game

"Execution is the game." – Gary Vaynerchuk, Entrepreneur, Author, Speaker, and Social Media Expert

Once the work is delegated, execution is an indispensable ingredient. Having your tasks structured is only the beginning. Goals are only met when executed.

What is execution exactly? Simply put, it is the act of carrying out a plan — following through.

Walking the walk, not just talking.

This chapter will be relatively brief as compared to the previous sections for a straightforward reason. And that reason is this book is for *do-ers*. You're here for a purpose. Either way, you want to change and better yourself. You're here to get things done. And that's precisely what this chapter is on — getting it done. Let me be clear, though — *you* are getting it done. This book won't just do it for you. Be mindful that you're in charge, but don't leave this book until your mind's full of ideas and preparation.

As a graduate of Florida Gulf Coast University's School of Entrepreneurship, I am extraordinarily appreciative of their faculty and staff. Especially Dr. Sandra Kauanui, the Director of the entire program.

FGCU's School of Entrepreneurship launched in Fall 2017 and has since grown to over 600 undergraduate students declared for the major, and hundreds more for the minor. I'm beyond grateful to have been the first Entrepreneurship major in fall 2017, experiencing the startup of the program itself.

According to The Princeton Review and Entrepreneur magazine, in the fall of 2019, FGCU was named the top college or university in Florida for undergraduate entrepreneurship studies.

It humbles me to know Dr. Kauanui personally. She and I had the opportunity to chat about this book, and she was kind enough to provide a statement for this chapter on execution. I asked her, *"How does Execution relate to one's ability to balance life and everything in it?"* Dr. Kauanui response:

"I believe Execution is extremely important to one's ability to balance life and everything that they want to do. Just thinking about or making a list of the items that need to be done doesn't make it happen. I have found in my own life that if I set clear and reasonable goals and hold myself accountable to complete these on a timely basis, I am better able to balance my work and family life.

I have managed to raise a family of four as a single mom for many years while running a successful business, which I eventually sold after 22 years. I then completed a Ph.D. in 4 years while starting a Center for Family Business at George Washington University. I have recently had the pleasure of starting and growing the School of Entrepreneurship at FGCU. All my accomplishments would not have been possible without using a process of planning and execution. In order to accomplish the successes in my life, I first needed a plan and then an execution plan which would allow me to achieve my goals in a timely manner. Without a strategy and an execution of the plan, it is tough to balance one's life. There are times it is necessary to focus on specific aspects of your life, but without taking action to complete what is needed, the mountain of responsibilities continues to grow and will only cause you to become more out of balance." – Sandra Kauanui, Ph.D., Program Director, Entrepreneur, and Professor

The real separation of a *significant* man or woman from average is their ability to follow through. They do what they say they're going to do.

At this point, you've identified your strengths, you've prioritized your goals, and delegated weaknesses to a team, and now it's time to separate the professionals from the amateurs.

So much of execution is having pride in your work. Are you proud of what you're doing? I certainly would hope so. After all, you're following your mission and vision statement.

When you have pride and passion, what you're striving for will come naturally to you. Not *easily*, but *naturally*. You'll expect it — at least most of the time, if you're *genuinely* invested in your work. You'll be placing yourself in all of the right places, at the correct times, and supported by the right network of people.

One of the core fundamentals of being a great leader includes integrity, also known as standing firmly behind your life's moral principles. Correlating directly with having integrity is execution. The execution shows commitment to your work, and leaders share this commonality of performance and engagement. When you follow through with what you're doing, it reflects that you are true to your word, and you are dedicated to completing the job. When you're committed to finishing your work, you're going to execute. You will find ways to get it done, no matter the adversities.

Great leaders also think and communicate their course of action clearly and effectively. Let's use a great analogy with the former President of the United States, Woodrow Wilson. President Woodrow Wilson was once asked how long it took him to prepare his speeches, and his response is relevant to our concept of thinking and communicating clearly. *"That depends on the length of the speech,"* said Wilson. *"If it is a 10-minute speech, it takes me all of two weeks to prepare it; if it is a half-hour speech, it takes me a week; if I can talk as long as I want to, it requires no preparation at all and I am ready now."*

President Wilson understood the correlation between preparation for the duration of speaking to the effectiveness of his delivery. A very strategic approach — one that identifies Woodrow Wilson as a renowned leader.

The moral of this analogy is to think and communicate clearly to execute effectively.

"To me, ideas are worth nothing unless executed. They are just a multiplier. Execution is worth millions." – Steve Jobs, Business Magnate, Industrial Designer, Investor, and Media Proprietor

SELF ASSESSMENTS

90-Day, Daily Tracking of SMART Goals (Ch. 15 Example A).

"Innovation is rewarded. Execution is worshipped." – Eric Thomas, Ph.D., Motivational Speaker, Author, and Minister

For anyone who doesn't quite know Eric Thomas, he often speaks for athletic teams and is best known for his story about wanting to succeed as badly as you want to breathe. It goes a little something like this:

"There was a young man who, you know, he wanted to make a lot of money. And so he went to this Guru, right, and he told the Guru, 'You know I wanna be on the same level you're on.' And so The Guru said, 'If you wanna be on the same level I'm on, I'll meet tomorrow, at the beach, at 4 AM.' He's like, 'The beach? I said I wanna make money. I don't wanna swim.' Guru said, 'If you wanna make money, I'll meet you tomorrow. 4 AM.'

So the young man got there at 4 AM. He is all ready to rock n' roll. Got on a suit. You should have worn shorts. The old man grabbed his hand and said, 'How bad do you wanna be successful?' He said, 'Real bad.' The Guru said, 'Walk on out in the water.' So he walks out into the water. When he walks out into the water it goes waist deep, so he's like, 'This guy is crazy. I wanna make money and he got me out here swimming. I didn't ask to be a lifeguard. I wanna make money.' The Guru said, 'Come out a little further.' He walked out a little further. Then he had him right around the shoulder area. 'So this old man is crazy. He's making money, but he's crazy.' So The Guru said, 'Come on out a little further.' He came out a little further, and it was right at his mouth. My man said, 'I'm about to go back in. This guy is out of his mind.' So the old man said, 'I thought you said you wanted to be successful?'

He said, 'I do.' The Guru said, 'Walk a little further.' He came, dropped his head in, and held him down. The Guru had him held down and just before my man was about to pass out, The Guru raised him up. The Guru said, 'I have a question for you. When you were underwater, what did you want to do?' He responded, 'I wanted to breathe.' The Guru said, 'When you want to succeed, as bad as you want to breathe, then you'll be successful.'" – Eric Thomas, Ph.D., Motivational Speaker, Author, and Minister

Ladies and gentlemen, it is so important — a necessity — to execute your game plan, to put in the work. Sure, sometimes it does take sacrificing sleep.

We talked about the fundamentals of sleep, so not to confuse you right now, it is unquestionably still fundamental. But again, it is *how* you can balance this with your will to succeed. And it all comes down to how badly you want it. Sacrifice some sleep for success *without* sacrificing your health. This comes through effective time management, prioritization of your hours spent, and a disciplined sleep schedule that will still offer you a healthy amount of sleep.

Maybe you just need to get to bed sooner, and waking up earlier won't be an issue. I know far too many people who lay awake at night on their phones getting sucked into YouTube, Instagram, and TikTok blackholes. Are you one of those people? Be disciplined enough to put it away on the nightstand and shut your eyes. This is a great time to incorporate meditation to fall asleep quicker.

Execution takes practice and effort.

You must be willing to learn and be coachable, just as the young man turned to The Guru for help. Because without effort, things will never get done.

You get in return what you put in, over some time, though. We talked about this earlier in the book, and it remains true. Put in the work and execute it. Execute as badly as you want to breathe, and you will become successful. You will find a balance. The sooner you start, the sooner you will see the progress that you're longing for.

If nothing were executed, it would all be meaningless. You can write up the most elaborate plan of action and tell everyone about it, but unless you're following through on that plan, it is practically meaningless.

Once you've nailed down that plan of action, *go!* Move forward! Step by step, day by day. Earlier, I mentioned a book by the title of *"Zero to One,"* authored by Peter Thiel. Do yourself a favor and get that book when you can. It does an excellent job of contextualizing execution and the concept of moving zero to one, one to two, two to three.

ATHLETICS

Great examples of executing what you preach and practice are sports teams. They have their workouts, practices, and overall game plans. Unless that team executes, they're going to lose no matter how much practice they might have gotten in prior.

Execution does not always give you the win, but the lack thereof certainly will provide you with the loss. Athletics teaches many of us what we know about execution: winning with an effective game plan.

Because of athletics, I was taught execution and time management at an early age, especially football. We could practice and practice perfectly, but unless we executed and managed the clock on the field come game time, none of it mattered. We had one play, one down, and one chance to execute each time that whistle blew and the ball was snapped. I could hear my coach now, screaming on the field, *"Get your asses back to the huddle, and this time, execute the damn play!!!"* Great times. Appreciated times.

A schedule in a life full of activity that is executed makes for an ability to balance it all effectively. Otherwise, what are you even balancing? Thoughts? Ideas? Notes that are written on paper?

You need to execute to balance your life effectively. You may stumble a few times, as do we all, but that's inevitable just as weaknesses are inevitable. Pick yourself up and try again, execute again.

Fail forward, and you will still progress forward.

WRITE SOME NOTES

Let's take a few of those goals that you have written down, or are in your head, and design a course of action. Maybe write a few immediate to-dos that must get done for a goal — things that you can get started on right away to get the ball rolling. Do you have a style of game planning? If so, carry that over to these notes and transition it all together.

———————————————————————

———————————————————————

———————————————————————

———————————————————————

———————————————————————

———————————————————————

———————————————————————

———————————————————————

———————————————————————

———————————————————————

———————————————————————

———————————————————————

Execution relates to consistency. Great, so you've got the ball rolling. You've locked down your game plan, and you're beginning to execute.

Maybe you've seen a little progress, perhaps not. Do you stop since you've *executed* your plan? I mean, you saw some improvement, so it's over, right? Wrong. Very wrong. This, ladies and gentlemen, is where the beautiful concept of consistency comes into play.

You're playing the game; you're executing. But we live in a world of pay-to-play nowadays. And guess what your currency is. *Consistency.* Consistency is your currency.

In this next chapter, we'll discuss how and why remaining consistent in your game plan is vital in its accomplishment. And why the best of the best all share this commonality.

Let's move on.

Chapter Ten.
Consistency is the Currency

*E*xecution is the game, you're the player, so how often do you want to play? Remember, we're in a pay to play world.

Consistency is your currency. Consistency of *what you do*. Consistency of *how you do it*. Consistency of *when and how often you do it*.

We talked about the five "W's" and one "H." This again applies to consistency. Your who, what, when, where, why, and how, must remain consistent if you seek accomplishment.

If you start something and begin executing your game plan, but after a few weeks or months, you just give up, then the chances of your success are low.

Depending on what you're doing or trying to accomplish, it might take years of consistency, such as starting a company. Years. It takes years of consistent smart and hard work to reach a sustainable position, let alone to achieve true product-market fit and stable revenue.

Developing a strong relationship takes consistency, as well. Consistent love, attention, and quality time spent together. Consistency resides in everything that we do and strive to accomplish.

Inc. 5000 is a list of the fastest-growing companies in America with revenues accumulating well into the hundreds of billions. According to the 2019 Inc. 5000 listing, sitting proudly at rank #2666 is the Naples-based Pyure Brands. Pyure Brands provides its customers with natural alternatives to sugar and artificial sweeteners.

Their founder and CEO, Benjamin Fleischer, is a fellow FGCU Alumni and local entrepreneur, as well as someone I consider to be a friend. Ben and I had the chance to chat over the phone recently. During our conversation, I asked Ben, *"How does consistency relate to living a well-balanced life?"* His response was so raw and relatable. This is what Ben had to say:

"As anything does, when you get into a pattern of doing something over and over again, it becomes habitual.

Once you have that, you're in the right psyche and head-space — overall wellbeing of life.

Let's give examples. In the realm of brushing your teeth, you just do it; it's a habit. When I started meditating a few years ago and incorporated breath-work, part of my ritual would be to wake up, go outside, and get into my meditative state of mind. As with everything, the first few weeks are tough because you're implementing something new in life. But then it becomes habituated and I do it over and over and over again. At this point, you start seeing it as part of your life and no longer just a 'task' or 'to-do.'

I was able to connect the dots as we grew, but there was still a gap. My life and routine were so focused on that hardcore work schedule, and it was honestly slightly out of balance. Everything — including stress — became out of balance. So did my mental health. I was just grinding and began self-imploding. I was completely off balance and realized I had to make a shift in my life and focus on a disciplined, habitual, and well-balanced life through consistency. When I started understanding that and getting into the right headspace, that's when I was able to get more clarity around a lot of things. And then I began diving deeper into that headspace. That ability of self-awareness is also a significant aspect of finding the right headspace and shifting until you find that balance. If I'm treating my mind a certain way, I have to work at balancing.

If I miss a day of meditation, it throws me off. So again, going back to ritual and pattern, it's about taking that first leap — the first day then second and third day — until it becomes a habit. All of this brings your life together into a greater sense of wellbeing. I always make discipline a priority, just as I make habits and rituals a priority. From business to personal life, I prioritize being in the right headspace and circling it all back into my entire life. I'm off if I don't fulfill my consistent schedule because it's turned into such a habit. Everything is off for the day. It coexists with my body. Every single day, I get better at it too with practice and consistency. That goes with everything — you get better the more it's done. You begin to crave it. But like everything, you must work at it. Then you'll start seeing benefits, and you'll begin experiencing the results.

The way I was raised is that it's a 'sink or swim' world. My whole thought process in building my business was working 60 to 80-hour weeks, 7-days a week, to establish what Pyure Brands is today — an Inc. 5000 Fastest Growing Company and home-brand. It didn't come from the space of 'I'm not going to be successful, so why even bother.'

When I talk to entrepreneurs, I can tell if they're off balance. They come at me with all of this groundwork, but leave out the headspace. I tell them that they're going to burn out quickly and will do themselves and everyone around them, a disservice. Sometimes you must take a few steps back, and you'll find that precise streamlined balance. So again, it's work — your headspace, the health, and not just putting more and more information into your mind. You need time to take a step back and translate that information in a way that it becomes your narrative and not just information. It becomes your story adaptable by you. You need to balance your life to create that. You have to understand how the outside world translates into your narrative, your story.

We're living in this world where everyone wants to be an entrepreneur. But not everyone is made for it. To be a true entrepreneur, you've got to be a bit crazy. To put everything on the line and put your life on a belief system that what you're doing will undoubtedly work (even if it doesn't, it's about that mindset). I see a lot of people thinking that entrepreneurship is a game and is cool. No. It takes mastermind energy, time, and dedication. And you've got to be a bit mad. And that's okay to be. But you've got to recognize it. I've imploded. I've been there. Other people have too. And it's not necessarily from a place of being a Debbie Downer, but it is reality. You can have all of the money in the world, but still not be happy. Entrepreneurship is a very interesting world unlike any other. I like to talk about the real aspect of it all. It can be a lonely road — not everyone understands how you're feeling and what you're putting into it. So you've got to show up by yourself every single day, through problems and challenges, and clap for yourself when nobody is *watching. And at the end of the day, what matters is how consistent you are in your approach and what it is that you're spending your time doing. All of this to live a well-balanced life."* – Benjamin Fleischer, Entrepreneur and Advisor

Coming from a successful young entrepreneur, the importance of consistency is relevant in all aspects of life. Without a proper sense of consistency, you will likely find yourself burning out and exerting your resources in all of the wrong places.

From a healthy headspace to a well-crafted schedule, creating the well-balanced and consistent lifestyle that you want takes systematic methods day in and day out.

And for the entrepreneurs out there, it can not be stressed enough that a lack of consistency in your day-to-day will result in a hard crash and burn. Ben's life lessons shed light on a lot of what I struggled with as a young entrepreneur. Since practicing his preaching, I've found a much healthier and stable sense of balance.

To be exact, it takes 26 days to build habits and 90 days to build lifestyles. So for the next month, decide on a practice you want to implement into your life. A proper eating schedule, a particular time spent with your spouse or friends, maybe getting back into the gym. To build this motive into a habit, it takes at least 26 days of consistency.

Now, if you're looking to go plant-based (vegan), partner with your friends on a new endeavor, or become a fitness fanatic, then you're looking at about 90 days of consistent work and effort applied to turn those into lifestyles.

SELF ASSESSMENTS

26-day challenge and 90-day challenge (Ch. 15 Example A). Hold yourself accountable and measure at the end to improve.

"Success isn't always about greatness. It's about consistency. Consistent hard work leads to success. Greatness will come." – Dwayne Johnson, Actor, Producer, and Serial Entrepreneur

Who doesn't love The Rock? Well, he's spot on when he says success isn't always about greatness. Yes, success *is* great, but getting there is not always about *being* great.

Success stems from one's ability to remain consistent with their craft, with their efforts. This hard work (and smart work) leads to success, and then greatness will come. Some people have it flipped around — that you *must* be fabulous to achieve success — like you *must* be rare or something. It's the other way around! Those who are consistent on their path to success will be the ones who achieve success when all is said and done. And as The Rock said, greatness will come.

Do you know what else will come with the ability to be consistent? Balance! When your efforts are consistent, you know *how much* you're balancing; you have a good understanding of the volume.

If you're working 80 hours one week while *trying* to balance two endeavors and family, but then the next couple of weeks you're taking most days off and hitting the clubs, it's going to be extremely difficult to find a life-balance amongst all of that chaos. When you're consistent, you're balanced.

The primary difference between successful entrepreneurs and those who are not is pure perseverance. They are not always far more skilled by nature; successful people are far more consistent and persistent in their execution. Now I know not everyone is an entrepreneur, but I find many commonalities between those who are and are not. You are crafting your life; you are creating value, seizing an opportunity, and solving problems. And the primary difference that will set aside those who succeed and those who do not will not be a lack of ability, but rather a lack of commitment and perseverance.

"Having a vision for what you want is not enough. Vision without execution is hallucination." – Thomas Edison, Inventor and Businessman

Practice what you preach and on a schedule. Are you catching onto a pattern yet? Follow through with whatever it is you do, yes everything, and make it a lifestyle.

Consistency is what got me to where I am today. I may be young but have accomplished quite a lot due to my abilities to execute and remain consistent — to persevere through difficult times and shortages of skill.

IT'S SIMPLER THAN YOU THINK

Simply try. Be the hybrid tortoise and hare.

Apply your best learning ability to practicing consistency. However it is you learn best and thoroughly, apply yourself to consistency, and set attainable goals at least 26 days out.

Oh, and one more thing — remove the excuses.

Seriously. This world has no room for excuses, and frankly, it does not care what your excuses are. I'm sorry to be the one to break it to you, but save that excuse, write it down on a notepad that nobody will see, then toss it in the trash. Why? Because nobody cares about your excuses. No excuses. Period.

"Around here, however, we don't look backward for very long. We keep moving forward, opening new doors, and doing new things, because we're curious and curiosity keeps leading us down new paths." – Walt Disney, Entrepreneur, Animator, Voice Actor, and Film Producer

An inconsistent schedule and life altogether will result in a "teeter-totter" or "hamster wheel" of life without balance. We discussed this already, so I hope by now you've heard me loud and clear, and that consistency in your life will allow for a well-balanced life.

To clarify, I'm not saying you need to live a repetitive life of the same things over and over. That's not the concept we're getting at here. Go sky diving and jump off cliffs, safely, for all I care. But if that's the type of work or fun that you do, be consistent with it! For all you know, GoPro and Redbull might be watching and want to sponsor you — but they're not going to sponsor someone who skydives once in a while. I can tell you that much.

Earlier in Chapter Six, a mentor of mine, Karl Gibbons, provided a thorough statement on setting goals and achieving them. He's back in this chapter to share some insights on developing your business and entrepreneurial skills. This is what Karl had to say:

"There are many books available to help develop your entrepreneurial and business skills, but all of TEMA's clients are given these two programs to watch as COMPULSORY VIEWING, as they cover everything any BOE (business owner entrepreneur) needs to know. Including communications, motivation, delegation, strategic and tactical planning, marketing, product development, cash flow, personnel, expansion, multi-location growth, profitability, systems and productivity, funding, time, and crisis management — any of these sound familiar?

'The West Wing' — an American serial political drama television series that was originally broadcast on NBC from September 22, 1999, to May 14, 2006. The series is set primarily in the West Wing of the White House, where the Oval Office and offices of senior presidential staff are located, during the fictitious Democratic administration of Josiah Bartlet. Whatever your political leanings look past those to the real management issues addressed in the series.

'The Newsroom' — an American television drama series that premiered on HBO on June 24, 2012, and concluded on December 14, 2014, consisting of 25 episodes over three seasons. The series chronicles behind-the-scenes events at the fictional Atlantis Cable News (ACN) channel. The story revolves around news anchor Will McAvoy who, together with his staff, sets out to put on a news show 'in

the face of corporate and commercial obstacles and their entanglements.'

Both The West Wing and The Newsroom were created and written by Aaron Sorkin, and as well as being great entertainment, I consider them to be some of the best business training videos available." – Karl Gibbons, Serial Entrepreneur, Motivational Speaker, Chairman, and Business Consultant

WRITE SOME NOTES

All right, my skydiving and cliff jumping ladies and gents, we're getting to the home stretch of the book. Pat yourself on the back for making it this far and putting up with my rants. Once you're done patting yourself on the back, jot down some notes about consistency and how you're going to apply it. Or better yet, what it is that you need to be more consistent with.

____

____

____

____

____

____

____

____

____

____

____

____

____

____

____

____

____

____

____

Consistency relates to accountability. But how can we truly measure consistency? For starters, the self-assessments that we've already reviewed throughout these previous chapters — especially the concept of 26-day habits and 90-day lifestyles.

Regardless, you always want to measure to get an idea of whether or not you're progressing. Just as I've mentioned in this book, it all starts with you. Taking accountability for yourself and your actions — not making excuses.

This next chapter will elaborate on accountability for everything it is that you do, holding yourself responsible for your entire life.

Let's move.

Chapter Eleven.
Holding Yourself Accountable – At All Times

One of the traits most lacking in people is the ability to hold themselves accountable. I've been guilty of it plenty of times — in fact, I still struggle with it sometimes as do we all.

I have my days of sleeping well past a reasonable hour or staying up far past a time to ensure quality rest and doing nothing about it to fix it. I also have my slip ups of not getting as much work done as I should, and instead, heading out on an unplanned beach day, excusing it because "I deserve it."

It is so important to hold yourself accountable at all times. Another interchangeable word for accountable is responsible. Do you take responsibility when something goes wrong or not the way you had planned it to go? Or do you just shrug it off, blame it on something or someone else, and move on? If you responded yes to the latter, you, my friend, have a lack of accountability, which is worrisome. But not to stress, this chapter will break down the importance of holding yourself accountable at all times, and for everything — even when you might think that some things are just out of your control, you still must hold yourself responsible.

A great book to read that sheds light on the noble acts of accountability is *"Flight of the Buffalo"* by James Belasco. There is an excellent leadership discussion within the book that stands out to readers and has been known to change the way leaders think. When finding yourself in situations where you've failed, made a mistake, or outside surroundings have a negative impact, you ask yourself, *"What is it that I did or didn't do that caused that to happen?" (Flight of the Buffalo, By James A. Belasco & Ralph C. Stayer, 1993, page 20).*

No matter how little your fault, you still put yourself in that position one way or another, and it's your responsibility to understand why. And to avoid it next time, make other decisions not to get put in that position.

If you continue to just blame other things, or people, on why you're not achieving, it's going to be extremely difficult in identifying what needs to be improved to reach that goal. You must be able to look at yourself in the mirror and know that you have failed; that you screwed up and admit it to yourself.

Do not just blame outside forces, because then you're not allowing yourself to grow. Get comfortable with failure, make it your friend, not your enemy. When failure becomes nothing more than the process of growth, your ability to be responsible strengthens, and your ability to balance lightens up.

It doesn't feel so heavy anymore when you stumble and can just chuckle at yourself like, *"Yup, I just screwed that up."* When your mindset is nurtured this way, you can ask yourself, *"What is it that I did wrong, and how can I improve so this doesn't happen again?"* Instead of *"Ah man, everything is over; it's all ___ fault, why did ___ have to ruin this for me?"* That is the wrong way to look at something — to perceive something. It gets you nowhere and left without improvement.

This especially goes for business owners. When you own a business and notably are the CEO, everything *is* your fault. Everything. Are customer support agents not acting right? Still your responsibility; you hired them and are lacking in training them properly. Sales team not meeting goals? Again your responsibility; you hired them and are lacking in preparing them properly. As Jim Collins put it in *"Good to Great,"* *"Look in the mirror and not out the window of the office to see who to blame."* It all comes down to you at the end of the day.

Failed the exam because you don't think the teacher gave enough preparation? Still, your fault for not taking responsibility for ensuring you were on top of the curriculum. Your friend got you into trouble for something they did? Again your fault for putting yourself in that position and being in the same environment. And the same goes for every one of us as individuals.

I was reading a few blogs one afternoon, and to my pleasant surprise, one of them was on the subject of taking responsibility for actions. The story is of four college students. It goes like this:

"One night, four college students were out partying late at night and didn't study for the test which was scheduled for the next day. In the morning, they thought of a plan. They made themselves look dirty with grease and dirt. Then they went to the Dean and said they had gone out to a wedding last night and on their way back the tire of their car burst and they had to push the car all the way back. So they were in no condition to take the test.

The Dean thought for a minute and said they can have the re-test after three days. They thanked him and said they would be ready by that time.

On the third day, they appeared before the Dean. The Dean said that as this was a Special Condition Test, all four were required to sit in separate classrooms for the test. They all agreed as they had prepared well in the last three days.

The Test consisted of only two questions with a total of 100 Points.

1) Your Name ___________ (1 Points)

2) Which tire burst? ___________ (99 Points)

Options – (a) Front Left (b) Front Right
(c) Back Left (d) Back Right

Moral: be responsible, else you too will learn your lesson!"

Lose the excuses, lose the negativity, lose the victimization. Instead, accept that failures are inevitable and befriend them. It will make your ability to hold yourself accountable natural and result in improvements.

When you hold yourself accountable, you're entirely honest with yourself. When you're entirely honest with yourself, you know *where* and *what* needs to be improved.

If you can't even support yourself by holding yourself accountable when life hits the fan or falling short in your progress, how do you plan on growing? Nobody can save you but yourself, so own up to your efforts and hold yourself accountable. Be responsible. *"When shit hits the fan, are you just going to sit there and let it spray all over you, or are you going to get up and unplug the fan? Unplug the fan!"* The wise words of a great friend of mine, Robert Swensen.

Find a mirror when something bad happens, and the person you see, it's their fault (hint: it's you). I know, I know, it sounds aggressive and that I'm attacking you personally. I promise that I'm not — just another chapter of being raw and real. I guess you can call me *a realist*. Allow me to explain further.

You put yourself in that environment; you chose to be with them, you allowed yourself to be influenced, you thought it was a good idea, yadda yadda yadda. No matter which way you try to spin it, it begins with you and some decision you made or didn't make, so take responsibility.

Let me clarify that whatever failure or bad situation that might've happened, it's okay. I'm not trying to say it's the end of the world because you screwed up. It's the complete opposite of that. I'm saying that you screwed up, *but* it's okay, things will be okay.

But for them to be okay and to improve, you must hold yourself accountable and learn from the mistakes. The same goes for successes as well.

When you succeed, take accountability and humble yourself because of it. Have yourself a slice of "humble pie," as Swensen has put it. If you won, accept that and smile with confidence. The same accountability will allow you to understand why it is you succeeded and what you need to continue to do moving forward.

It goes both ways, and the universal message of accountability is that it allows you to know what needs to be worked on, improved, and made better, all to become the best version of yourself.

This is the accurate measurement of your goals being met or not — success being accomplished or falling short. There is always room for improvement, so you need to admit where those rooms are. Where those empty spaces are and that it's *you* who needs to fill the void.

SELF ASSESSMENTS

While tracking assessments, own up to failures, and review at the end of each week. Ask a friend/ housemate to be your accountabillibuddy.

"It is wrong and immoral to seek to escape the consequences of one's acts." – Mahatma Gandhi, Lawyer, Anti-Colonial Nationalist, and Political Ethicist

If you've done something wrong, have fallen short, or things just didn't go as planned, you must not avoid those results just because you don't like them.

Accepting the consequences for your actions puts you in a place of control. Control over *what* happened, *why* it happened, and *how* you're going to fix it.

You remove that control from yourself when you attempt to escape the consequences. Own up to them, take them head-on, and the rest will get better and brighter, and your questions will be answered.

In the context of business culture, accountability plays such an important role inside of the C-suite. Here at Fieldr, we utilize the Entrepreneurial Operating System tools for our weekly leadership meetings and monthly board meetings.

I was fortunate to be introduced to this concept by someone who is easily considered an expert in this field of accountability, Ross Gibbs. As an official Certified EOS Implementer™, Ross has experience working with businesses of all sizes, for-profit and nonprofit, worldwide. What does EOS mean? *"EOS®, the Entrepreneurial Operating System® is a comprehensive business system, integrating a holistic business model with a complete set of simple business tools and proven busi-*

ness processes to align and synchronize all the pieces of your business to produce the results you want" (https:// www.eosworldwide.com/). Ross was willing to contribute, I asked him, *"How does holding oneself accountable relate to the ability to live a well-balanced life?"* Ross answered with:

"Accountability is a result of creating quality habits that bring the results we desire. I will give you two examples of this. I call these my AM and PM bookends. These are habits I created at the end and beginning of each day.

Example 1

I always say your best day starts the night before. I have a digital sunset one hour before bed, where I turn off all the blue light and inputs so I can ready myself for a good night's sleep. When we manage our energy, we can show better as our best selves. That's accountability based on desired results. Consistently doing the mundane is typically what gets you what you want. It's not the fireworks and parades that everyone thinks. That's a myth.

Example 2

The other thing I do is I have a morning routine where I focus on three areas of what I want to be in the world. I call this the big three times two exercises. I got this from my Optimizer Coach, Brian Johnson. The areas I focus on are energy, work, and love. There are many other areas one can focus on, but I find these three cover almost everything we do. Energy is about eating, body movement, and sleep. Work is obvious. Love is our connections with the world, our friends, our family, and our significant other. So, we have time management. Then we have energy management that drives our time. There is higher management that drives our energy and time, and that is virtue management.

So, here is how the big three times two exercise works: I first determine my identity in my energy, work, and love. Our identity is crucial because it will move us to start doing the disciplined things we want to do so we can be more accountable. Here is my identity in energy: I am active and radiantly healthy. My identity in work is, I am a world-class coach. My identity in love is, I am a great man. These may sound boastful, but they are not because these statements set us up to how we want to show up to the world. Here is where virtue management comes in. I then read my virtues in each of three areas. Think of virtues as moral excellence. Aristotle and Greeks mastered this concept. Here are my virtues. Energy, I am committed and take ownership. I am wise, authentic, and courageous. I am kind, generous, patient, and encouraging. I then pick one thing I am going to do in each of these three areas each day. These three things have to happen before I do anything else, usually before any digital inputs or interruptions from others. My big three times two today were; energy-workout, work-update all client session pre-sentations, and love-send an encouraging note to each of the kids.

The point I am making is when we know ourselves and understand how we want to show up in the world, we become more accountable to ourselves and others. We live a more balanced life because we are clear on who we are, and understand the gift of presence, whether we are at work or home." – Ross Gibbs, Certified EOS Implementer™, Consultant, Entrepreneur, and Mentor

Life changes for the better when you take full accountability, even if it may not seem like it right away. Think of it as a simple way of adjusting internal emotion and perspective.

No need to feel bad for yourself and sulk, and most certainly no reason to look at the failure as *the end*. Life truly does become brighter when you befriend failures, and you can naturally take accountability. Things suddenly appear as they indeed are, no mask made of excuses and blame. And suddenly there is no room left for those excuses in your life; they become a way of the past. Where you see raw, you see reality.

Owning up to mistakes or successes puts the clarity in direction; it puts you in the driver seat and in full control of what happens next. If you're making excuses left and right and can't be responsible for your actions, you're just balancing a bunch of nonsense. And that gets heavy.

WRITE SOME NOTES

What are some things in which you need to start taking more accountability? Maybe it's something in the workplace or at home. Be honest with yourself and take some notes on what it is that it's time to be responsible for and not always avoid when it doesn't go your way.

____

____

____

____

Accountability relates to coachability and constructive criticism. Now we can't expect to know all of the answers — at least all of the right answers. And so that is why we take accountability in the first place. But secondly, it's essential to be open to how you can better yourself and the situation.

In this next chapter, we're going to discuss the importance of coachability and the overall acceptance of constructive criticism from others.

Chapter Twelve.
Coachability and Constructive Criticism

You can't expect to be perfect, so be willing to learn from mistakes and others. We touched on this in the very first chapter. Nobody is perfect. We're all imperfect in our ways, in our own lives.

So with that said, there's always room for improvement and growth. But not all lessons learned must come from hardship or failure. Although failure and difficulties are a phenomenal learning lesson and place of growth, there are other ways to become a better version of yourself.

For instance, you took the leap by reading this self-education/self-help book, and my hopes are you're able to pull some lessons learned from myself and the great leaders included in this book. The fact that you even bought this book, or were given it, shows that you already do carry this ability to be coachable and to accept constructive criticism. When you've been able to take responsibility for what happens to you, you open the doors for learning.

Accept constructive criticism; take the feedback given to you with a grain of salt. By definition, constructive criticism is "the process of offering valid and well-reasoned opinions about the work of others, usually involving both positive and negative comments, in a friendly manner rather than an oppositional one." More often than not, the feedback or lesson that someone is trying to bestow upon you is because that person cares about you and wants to see you do better. Not everyone who has advice for you is doing it because they feel superior to you.

Those you choose to surround yourself with are more often than not giving you constructive criticism to *better* what you might be trying to accomplish.

Just think of athletic coaches and their players. A good coach does not yell at or instruct players to put them down nor to make them feel inferior. The coach wants to see the team succeed, grow together and individually, and to win. And it often takes doing precisely what their position is, coaching!

Feedback in the critical scheme of things is how you fail forward and learn your lessons. There's an honest concept that when someone stops giving you input on how to become a better you, it's most likely because they've given up on you. When people take their time to offer their insight and constructive criticism, they care about your wellbeing and want to see you win.

Often, we jump to emotion when receiving this feedback: anger, offense, resistance. Sometimes we may even retaliate verbally, out of that spurred emotion. A few steps for understanding the situation that has helped me open my eyes to feedback are as follows.

1. Take a deep breath, and if it's truly bothering you a lot, take a brief moment to step away and find the right headspace without giving a knee jerk reaction.

2. Accept what emotion it is you're feeling and know that it is only temporary.

3. Ask questions to the other person. The "W's" and "H" so you can get the best sense of understanding the situation.

4. Ask what you can do better, and if the other person might be willing to help.

5. Give thanks for the feedback and watch as the other person reiterates that they are here to help and want to see you succeed.

I was very fortunate to learn the concept and importance of constructive criticism and coachability at an early age. I'm lucky to have been surrounded by parents and people that always pushed me to do better. Surround yourself with those types of people who will be honest and look out for your wellbeing. Again, these people are telling you this because they genuinely care about you.

For me, coachability came through a variety of sports as I was growing up. My football, baseball, soccer, lacrosse, and basketball coaches all played a role in my ability to be coached and accept their advice on becoming a better athlete, teammate, and man altogether. The discipline behind athletics will make or break a person and always push them to their full potential if they're willing to be coached.

Constructive criticism came primarily from my dad. I can hear him now saying those two words. Off the field, I would be resistant to people's advice and critiques. Especially my dad's who *"didn't know what he was talking about."* HA! I laugh at myself now, just typing that knowing that's how I used to feel. The truth is, he knew *exactly* what he was talking about while I figured I knew everything.

I would push back, I'd let my ego get the best of me, and it'd slow me down and slow my progress. You see, improvement is seen most where there is a failure. When I wouldn't listen, though, I would fail without moving forward. My ego got in the way of hearing clearly and therefore not thinking clearly, not recognizing the fact he/they're trying to help me.

It didn't take long for me to get comfortable with constructive criticism, and since then, it has been my best friend. Failure and constructive criticism are two of my best friends, and because of that, I've been able to surround myself with a network of expert experience.

One of the many great attributes to the Legacy Leadership Forum is getting to know some incredible professionals living here in the Southwest Florida community.

Of these many great professionals is Eric Gallus, the CEO of Premier Plus Realty, based in Naples, FL. Premiere Plus Realty is the recipient of multiple awards including People's Choice Winner for Best Commercial, Gulfshore Best of Business for Best Small Company and Best Commercial, and most recently recognized as one of Florida's Top 50 Brokerages in the State by Florida Realtors. Sharing conversations with Eric is something I find invaluable; his authentic entrepreneurial personality inspires me. He was kind enough to offer some words of encouragement for this book. I asked Eric, *"How does Coachability and Constructive Criticism relate to the ability to live a well-balanced life?"* Eric said to me,

"You have to be willing to change in order to grow. Pride can leave you bitter and uncoachable. If your heart truly desires to find balance, then you have to constantly accept failures as opportunities to learn from. Don't be too

hard on yourself, but also don't waste the time you've been given. Having a teachable heart has been one of the most rewarding aspects of my personal and professional journey. Nothing will break the pillar of pride more than receiving real wisdom from those before you and walking daily with a posture of humility." – Eric Gallus, Entrepreneur, Chief Executive Officer, and Real Estate Broker

Learn from mistakes and always listen.

The power of listening is often always more effective than the power of speaking. And not just listening, but rather active listening. Active listening involves observing the speaker's behavior and body language to deeper understand what is being said. These following six simple steps have been constructive for me in applying active listening:

1. Be an absorber, not just an observer.
2. Let the silence do the work.
3. Ask follow-up questions.
4. Gauge the feelings.
5. Test your understanding.
6. Take notes.

Always listen before you speak, and be aware of the quietest individual in the room because they often know the most.

A lot of it starts with losing the ego! It helps to look up to people who share a culture that you want to align with. You don't need to become them, but you can model their behavior and success, just like we discussed earlier in this book.

All great leaders are known to ask questions and not be the ones always talking. According to Nolen and his proven leadership development methods, *"The essence of leadership itself is knowing how to ask the right questions."* Notice how he mentioned the *right* questions, not just a ton of questions. Although more is better in some cases, the higher the quality of the question, the better.

SELF ASSESSMENTS

Breakdown who has your best interests. Analyze who you trust in your life. Practice accepting criticism and hear out the provider for their reasons (Ch. 15 Example B).

"My best skill was that I was coachable. I was a sponge and aggressive to learn." – Michael Jordan, NBA Team Owner and Former Professional Basketball Player

As we discussed, sports is a whole world of coachability and constructive criticism in itself, similar to the workplace with a boss and their employees. In the context of athletics, Michael Jordan — arguably the best basketball player of all time or at least one of — accredits his world-renowned skills to being coachable. This is coming from an all-time great, an NCAA and NBA Champion, an American icon for athletes and like-minded people.

MJ's burning desire for learning turned him into a six-time national champion. We even discussed the concept of being a sponge — being a forever learner. When you're continually learning and being coached on how to become better, you're taking the edge on the competition and putting yourself in a winning position.

Want to hear the best part about MJ's story? He was cut from his high school basketball team in 1978 for being too short and not capable of dunking yet — not skilled enough. Michael Jordan himself, cut from the team. The same Jordan that is now worth $2.1B as of 2020 according to Forbes — talk about being coachable, taking criticism, and molding it into success.

The power of fitness.

Never overlook any type of athletic-related activity and the mental power it delivers. Might I encourage you to get involved in a club sport, a community league, a gym class? Whatever it is that is available to you, take advantage of it and go into it with an open-mind of coachability and willingness to accept constructive criticism. Allow for trainers to guide your activity, and the same goes for academia or industry insight. Allow mentors, advisors, or your colleagues to guide your actions or endeavors in the right direction. I'm a firm believer that athletics stabilizes one's ability to learn by putting you in the right style environment.

One of Fieldr's Advisory Board Members, Steven Becker, is someone I look up to for coaching and direction. He's the former Senior VP of Human Resources for international corporations such as Honeywell, Office-Max, Signet Jewelers, and Fujitsu. As an executive coach himself, Steve carries a strong sense of constructive advice and support for people, and he was willing to share his insights with us. I asked Steve, *"What is the relativity between accepting constructive criticism/feedback and balancing everything in life?"* His response:

"As an executive coach, I interact with individuals that are focused on improving their leadership and interpersonal skills and abilities. Oftentimes the process includes having the executive and their colleagues participate in a 360-degree assessment that provides the executive with feedback and insight as to how they and others perceive their behavior. The feedback an executive receives usually includes strength areas and constructive feedback on their weaknesses. Both types of feedback are beneficial because it provides input from others on what the individual does well and where they need to improve. It is not unusual for the feedback to uncover a 'blind spot' in the person's per-

ception of themselves. The feedback that uncovers a blind spot can be incredibly eye-opening for the person and, if acted upon, creates an opportunity for personal change that can positively impact one's life and relationships. So, in short, if a person listens to and accepts constructive feedback and then works to address specific behaviors, their presence can be positively transformed.

I'll share a story to illustrate this point. I once worked with a very bright high achieving executive that held extremely high-performance standards for himself and for everyone around him, including his employees, peers, and family. He was what most people would describe as 'wound tight.' Through constructive feedback and examining his blind spots, the executive came to realize that he was sabotaging his work and personal relationships by the way he interacted with and treated others. Through a lot of personal reflection and hard work to change his attitudes and behavior, his relationships at work and home were substantially improved. He became less judgmental of others around him and learned to better balance his emotions, attitude, behavior, and life." – Steven Becker, Executive Coach and Advisor

Nobody can naturally balance everything that they take on. It takes learning, practice, and it takes coaching. When you're open-minded to coaching and constructive criticism, you're elevating your chances of success.

I'm not saying that you *need* a life coach or business coach, but taking the steps in that direction, such as reading self-education or self-help books like this one, will make a huge difference.

But, I also *do* encourage exploring the possibility of a coach. Having a personal mentor or business mentor is invaluable. I have one personal mentor and a few business mentors, including Fieldr's Advisory Board. Every night I rest secure knowing I learned something new, and further exposed myself to a world of success.

Give yourself the pleasure of being coachable, it will answer a lot of the questions and doubts you might have within, and it all plays a role in your ability to live a well-balanced life.

Just like this book is about a well-balanced life, find yourself a mentor who has a strong understanding of balance! This world is full of knowledgeable people — why not elevate your life by surrounding yourself with those who can tell you and show you what it takes to win?

WRITE SOME NOTES

First, I encourage you to write down a few people who you might find to be fitting mentors. Mentors that align with the style of life you want to live; chances are they've made the mistakes that you want to avoid, and they'll be more than happy to share how to do so.

Write their names down and make it a priority to contact them within the next 12 hours — we don't want this to slip your mind.

Second, write down a few things that you'd like to get some extra help on! If you can't seem to pinpoint who would be the best mentor, at least you know what it is you should be looking for in a mentor.

____

____

____

____

Coachability and constructive criticism relate to integrated balance. All right, we're three chapters away from being done! You're just about there. I hope by now, you've captured a strong sense of the courses of action and adjustments that need to be made. Or maybe this has reaffirmed you're doing it all right!

This next chapter is one of my favorites. The title might be a bit confusing, but you'll see what I mean by "integrated balance." Just know that being coachable has everything to do with building your well-balanced life.

Moving on.

Chapter Thirteen.
Integrated Balance – Not 50/50

We can look at this concept of integrated balance in a few different ways. For starters, integrated balance can be understood as the ability to balance both growth and learning, simultaneously. This is similar to the concept of working *in* your business as well as *on* your business.

Relating to our previous chapter, to achieve balance, one must be coached by those who are better, faster, more reliable, and more stabilized.

We mentioned taking advice with a grain of salt, and to elaborate on that, I am referring to only adjusting to those who have done what you're about to do and have done it successfully. It's wise to filter what you're coached on rather than jumping to a decision based on something somebody told you. Take their advice, filter it, and strategically apply it to *your* course of action.

This is the ability to grow independently, all while learning, relative to our integrated balance concept.

You're balancing what you're already taking action on, as well as balancing external advice and expertise that you learn along the way. All this with the purpose of the most effective growth.

There's a more profound way we can break down and perceive this integrated balance concept.

F**K THE 50/50 BALANCE

It's a trap. Hear me out.

I know that many people hear this "work/life" balance ideology and might have even found success in it. I'm here to defy that and push its buttons, and hopefully open you up to a new way of looking at balance altogether. An *integrated* balance instead.

The 50/50 balance leads you into the rat race, finding yourself trapped by decisions and differences. Choices of where attention must be placed, where your efforts and resources must be placed, and often these decisions are split with one side of the 50/50 being focused on more than the other.

These splits in decisions, and frankly splits of yourself, are what then lead to being trapped by differences. Differences in the amount of time spent, where it's spent, who it's spent with, and why you're even indifferent. This type of balance creates two worlds that you must live in, and tends to cause stress, mixed emotions, and even doubt whether you're doing the right thing. Let me break this down even further with a specific example.

Let's say you're working your full-time job in the administrative department for a local company. You get paid decent money, enough to pay the bills, and after all, it's work. But you're not too happy at this job; it doesn't bring you excitement. You also happen to be mentoring/tutoring students, which is a huge passion of yours — you love the education industry. Beyond that, you're a big fan of going out with friends.

You've built this structure where you're working X amount of hours in the admin role, then after hours, you're working Y amount of hours mentoring, and then spending Z amount of hours with friends. You feel like this formula of time management is going to work out.

That is until the day-job begins to stress you out more and more since you're not fully invested in it, but you tell yourself it's a job. The tutoring sessions become a bit of a drag because now you're overwhelmed with office work from earlier in the day. Then comes a night out with friends, but at this point, you're just too exhausted from trying to make this work/life balance successful.

You even thought this perfect formula was going to give you the structure that you wanted. So what went wrong?

For starters, the job. Why are you working at a company where you don't enjoy it entirely nor find excitement in going to? Just because it pays? There's your first problem — and it's a problem that a lot of people share.

There's no reason to be balancing something that has no meaning or real purpose in your life. Your passion is in education, helping students. Might I suggest getting a job within a school institution where you can pursue your passion while being paid? Or starting your own consulting business? And now you've just effectively integrated a salary with passion for work. Because you've done this, your schedule is alleviated of pressure, allowing you to pick and choose when you want to head out with those friends of yours. This is just one *very specific* example, but I can imagine it applies to many readers to some capacity.

Too often, people get jobs just for the money while also trying to pursue what their passion is on the side. What sense does that make??? It's the 21st century! Turn your passion into your job!

Balance is a full-time, *100%* art form, as should be your passions and interests in life.

This is where you'll often see individuals working for the weekend. It kills me when I hear people say they can't wait for the week to be over.

Why? Why not live for all seven days of the week? Why not love Monday?

People think this is impossible because they have fallen victim to this 50/50 balance where they feel work is supposed to be different from outside life.

That's crazy! Lose the excuses; love and live every day of what you do.

Allow me to clarify what I mean by "live." No, I don't mean going out and getting into trouble while shouting, *"You only live once!"* Preferably, truly enjoying and appreciating what you do, day in and day out.

Integrated balance is about fulfilling passions and dreams by building your life on that foundation. Suddenly you realize that you only die once, so live *every* day.

A day of work will not feel like "work" when you love what you do and are passionate about it. Often this creates an integrated balance of work, personal hobbies, family and friends, etc.

And for everyone who's overly obsessed with money and losing sanity because of it, here's a reminder: you do not die with the money, you'll die with regret of not doing what you truly loved with who you love. *Mind blown*

"The person passionate about what he or she is doing will outwork and outlast the guy motivated solely by making money." – Reid Hoffman, Tech Entrepreneur, Venture Capitalist, and Author

When solely motivated by making money, and as much of it as possible, people tend to get distracted by shiny objects; it's the nature of most humans.

We see a thousand tweets, posts, and comments about ways of "getting rich quick" almost every day, and sometimes a few will get our attention.

People take job offers solely because the salary or hourly rate is higher than the other offer when, in reality, the other is a more meaningful and impactful opportunity. It's this self-destructive vision that "money will solve all problems," and that creating a life around what means most to us should come second to money. Flip that around, and you've got your winning formula; create an experience that is filled top to bottom with what matters most to you and is most impactful, and the money will follow.

All the while, you'll be designing this integrated balance between everything that you do from sunrise to sundown. Do what you love, and you'll love what you do.

Trust me, I'm a *huge* fan of money. But more importantly, I'm an even bigger fan of doing what makes me happy every waking minute, no matter how many commas.

SELF ASSESSMENTS

Time allocation. The breakdown should result in a 90% success rate with a 10% flexibility rate at the end of each month (Ch. 15 Example C).

Breakdown what you're doing and when you're doing it. Remove unnecessary tasks that are hanging over your head. Pay down bad debt hanging over your head. Analyze your current job. Ask yourself if what you're doing aligns with your culture (Ch. 15 Example F).

"If you live for the weekends and vacations, your shit is broken." – Gary Vaynerchuk, Entrepreneur, Author, Speaker, and Social Media Expert

Gary said it, not me!

But seriously, if you do live for the weekends, you need to reconsider what it is you're doing during the weekdays. If for five days of the week you're looking forward to when it's over, you're definitely not pursuing something you love or are passionate about. You're most likely just in it for the money, for the "drink vouchers on the first and fifteenth of the month," as my mentor has put it. And when you're just in it for the money, your balance is never going to be achieved; instead, you'll be running in circles of paychecks, stress, and lack of fulfillment. Whether you see that now or not isn't up to me. But Steve Jobs has something to say: *"Your work is going to fill a large part of your life, and the only way to be truly satisfied is to do what you believe is great work. And the only way to do great work is to love what you do. If you haven't found it yet, keep looking. Don't settle. As with all matters of the heart, you'll know when you find it. And, like every great relationship, it just gets better and better as the years roll on. So keep looking until you find it. Don't settle."*

Some people ask me to slow down because I'll just get on this passion-fueled train of speaking. I'll start talking very fast and pour out tons of information. Sure, I need to think and communicate clearly, but it's just my passion for everything I do. That's the reason for my 100% energy, Monday to Monday. Passion *is* my coffee — although I've never had a cup of it in my life (the coffee I mean). Will I ever change who I am and the energy that I carry? Absolutely not! Because that is *me*; that is the Connor Firmender who is always high on life.

During my final semester at Florida Gulf Coast University, while I was incubating Fieldr, I had the absolute pleasure of meeting a gentleman by the name of Geoff Evans. Since our initial meet, Geoff has been a Fieldr Advisory Board member alongside Karl Gibbons and Steve Becker. Without a doubt, Geoff has been a massive influence on my personal and company growth.

Although now retired and onto his independent endeavors, Geoff was once the Managing Partner for Boeing Ventures, Board Member of the Seattle University Business School, as well as President and CEO of Boeing Tapestry Solutions.

Given his exceptional contributions and engagement, he's had a lot of experience with sustaining an integrated balance. I asked Geoff, *"What is your perspective on having an integrated-balanced life versus a work/life balance?"* Geoff responded:

"Connor, my perspective is that in pursuit of work-life balance, it is always best (and more realistic) to pursue an integrated or (I always liked to call it) 'blended' lifestyle. For example, when I was working and my daughter was growing up, as often as possible, I tried to take her and my wife on business trips with me (especially the international ones). Rather than spending over a week away, and when I returned from the trip trying to 'balance' things with a full week with them, I could instead achieve some 'balance' by including them on the trip and thereby 'blending' my two worlds. An added advantage to

this kind of approach is that it gives your family some insight into your work world that they might otherwise not get. And a personal benefit for me is that it helped me to make a reality, the dream/wish my daughter told me about at age 6 (she wanted to visit all of the continents before the age of 21). That realized dream (and experiences we had on those trips) is now a permanent part of her life and a significant portion of my legacy as a working father. And that is all due to my decision, 25 years ago, to pursue work/life balance in a blended (or integrated) way." – Geoff Evans, Senior Aerospace Executive and Business Advisor

It will get hard.

It is *always* challenging when you're pushing outside of your comfort zone and pushing your limits. So you must be passionate about what you do, or the chances are you're going to burn out sooner than later.

In Chapter One, we saw another Steve Jobs quote referencing how important it is to have passion for what you do because it most definitely will get hard. And without that passion, most rational people will give up.

HAVE A MANTRA OR TWO

My mantras that guide my daily life:
1. Live with purpose, love with passion.
2. Do what you love, love what you do.

Have your mantra. A mantra can be a couple of words, a phrase, a sentence, or a statement. Typically, they're a shorter length and can apply to your life's culture — the way you live.

A personal mantra is specifically defined as "an affirmation to motivate and inspire you to be your best self." Have multiple reasons for your *why,* and you will naturally find your integrated balance of what's imperative and here to stay in your life.

I stumbled upon a phenomenal blog post by author Christy Wright. Christy also touched on some great ways that you can achieve this integrated life balance. Here's what Christy had to say.

"Here are five ways you can achieve life balance, too:

1. Do more now so you can do less later on. Just like in my example above, this has to do with recognizing that the season you're in now won't be the season you're in forever.

2. Speak up. Be honest with your boss, your coworkers, spouse, or extracurricular groups when you feel your plate is too full—and come with suggestions for practical alternatives. Don't be afraid to raise your hand and ask for help, because I guarantee they've been there before, too. Plus, most people like to feel like they're helping you.

3. Everything in your life is not equal. You need to give people, events, and (don't forget!) yourself importance by designating them your time. There's no 'right' order because your priorities are unique to you—but you should come up with a hierarchy. Having clear priorities will help reduce your stress, AND it will make decision-making much easier when you're pulled in multiple competing directions. And then you'll be empowered to…

4. Say 'No.' I love this quote by Warren Buffet: 'The difference between successful people and really successful people is that a really successful person says no to almost everything.' The truth is that your time is finite, and, by the way—it's yours. You don't just have the right to say no; you have the responsibility to say no. If you don't protect your time, no one else will.

5. Be 100% present. When you're at the softball game, be fully present for your kids—and don't let your mind wander to the thousand other things you 'should' be doing. When you're at the office, be all-in for your coworkers. When you're at the dinner table, dedicate your atten-

tion to your spouse. Treat your priorities like priorities, and everything else will fall into place."

Integrated balance is the *only* balance. So do your best to mold the life that you want, and by doing so, you will establish that integration and live a well-balanced life. To help you do this, I want to introduce you to the Wheel of Life.

Some of you might have seen it, some not. These eight pillars of life cover all that is in our lives, one way or another. Move through each pillar, scoring yourself on a one to ten scale. A well-balanced, well-integrated life will result in a similarity between all eight pillars and, hopefully, on the high end of the range. If one or some are far off from others — specifically lower than others — you have a strong sense of what requires more attention and effort. This assessment has worked well for me, and I hope it works well for you.

Give it a go.

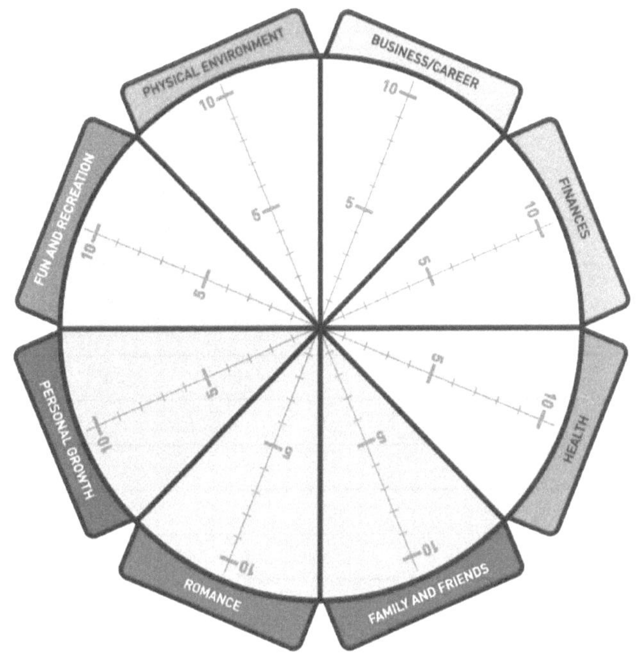

(https://www.mindtools.com/pages/article/new-HTE_93.htm)

WRITE SOME NOTES

What are your thoughts on this chapter? Maybe draw yourself a T-chart or some form of a list where you can compare and contrast what you're doing in life that is both for your passions and then for the paychecks. Are there any commonalities that can be molded into one another? I hope this chapter has inspired you to be entirely honest with yourself about where you're putting your efforts and whether they're in the right places. Remember, integrated balance will originate from pursuing passions.

246

Integrated balance relates to life management. In the next section, we're going to tie everything we've discussed nicely together in a bow, and then send you on your way with the gift of self-knowledge.

This next chapter is about managing life altogether. As we've already said, this is all much easier said than done, and sometimes life will throw curveballs at you. This chapter is how to manage those curveballs, how to manage change.

Homestretch!

Chapter Fourteen.
Life Management

"If you're waiting until you feel talented enough to make it, you'll never make it." – Criss Jami, Poet, Essayist, Existentialist Philosopher, Songwriter, and Designer

$\mathcal{F}$rankly, this chapter is just another way to look at the concept of balancing life; to tie this whole book together and send you on your way with inspiration and a new mindset of winning. This chapter is all about management — life management to be specific.

As did this book, managing your life begins with you and your internal emotions — your emotional intelligence. If you can apply what we discussed in the first chapter, you're certainly going to build a strong foundation for managing everything that comes your way. When you've found control over those emotions that sometimes tend to run wild, you've discovered power altogether. You've put yourself in the driver seat of your life, and that's precisely where you belong.

Following your emotional intelligence is both your internal and your external perspectives — how you view yourself as a person and contributor, as well as how you view the outside world.

It's no secret we live in a chaotic world nowadays. There's no need to list the array of tragedies and wrongdoings that we regularly see on the news and social media — it's all evident. So there's no shame that it is often difficult to control that perspective; our imagination loves to run wild, and opinions are formed of everything and everyone.

But it's when you've grasped hold of those perspectives that you're able to see everything for what it truly is, no sugar-coat and no mask — including the way you view yourself. Life becomes authentic, transparent, raw, and much easier to deal with, much easier to manage.

We also discussed the vital roles of life's fundamentals. The proper sleep schedule. Proper nutritional habits. And the adequate amount of love, both for yourself and the significant others around you. Stick to these, and within a month, you'll be unrecognizable from when you weren't abiding by these principles.

Life becomes much more natural and smoother to manage when you're in the right headspace. And that's exactly what these fundamentals will do for you.

Find those strengths, identify, and proudly accept those weaknesses. I promise that when you increase your focus on natural strengths and skillsets, life will start progressing in leaps and bounds. Your steps will become strides; your hops become leaps.

And never feel as though you're limited to what you can do with those strengths. If you're someone who is not too fond of what it is that you're naturally good at, I encourage you to explore the world of options that are at our fingertips. I bet that you'll find even more ways of applying those same natural skills. And if those options don't exist, well, then here's an excellent opportunity for you to pioneer what hasn't been done before. After all, we see the most success in life when we've been able to claim a niche or a specialty in our work and efforts. So stand out, and stand tall.

Your mission and vision will shed light on what needs to be balanced and managed, so I encourage you to have those written and remembered. But most importantly, apply it to your life.

You have the chance to design the life that you want and dream of, so slap your label on it with a mission and vision, and you'll find much greater ease in accomplishing it.

I'm not saying it will ultimately be easier; remember Denzel's quote — that ease is a greater threat to you than hardship. But, it certainly helps your case when you can alleviate unnecessary pressure by recognizing the mission in advance.

Just like our soldiers are briefed on their mission and vision of success before being sent off on a mission, I encourage you to do the same before sending yourself off into our world's depths. Manage your life with that direction, and be sure to enjoy the ride. It's always said that the journey is more impactful than the destination, and I couldn't agree more. On this note of enjoying the journey and not just the destination, I highly encourage you to read *"The Alchemist"* by Paulo Coelho.

Train the mind *and* train the body. Athletics and general exercise will be such a benefit to your mental strength and ability to manage everything in life. Fitness also exposes you to managerial tactics and discipline, so make it a part of your life, and you'll see the impact it will have on your work and overall performance.

Being able to balance academics, work, and fitness also *creates* leaders and managers, so when you've found your rhythm of balance, look to integrate that style of life. Even if it be morning/evening runs, weight lifting, etc., it all matters and will all have a positive impact.

Follow through with your words, and take accountability for successes and failures. Our chapters of execution, consistency, and accountability should have covered this reasonably well. Until you are sincere and honest to yourself, you'll be managing a fantasy and spinning in a hamster wheel. Be honest with yourself no matter what outside opinions you might receive and any failures you might endure. If you stay honest with yourself, then nothing can defeat you or bring you down. It's an ability to level the playing field in life and see everything right in front of you, rather than looking down and hanging your head.

SELF ASSESSMENTS

Breakdown everything you have going on, everything (Ch. 15 Example C).

Sit with a personal mentor (if you don't have one, get one) and breakdown everything with him/her. Gain insights/experience into life management and decisions (Ch. 15 Example E).

"Know what your path looks like, know where your destinations might be. But most importantly, lay that next brick as perfectly and as finely as you possibly can. And then the next one. And then the next one. And so, you will then have your path to your destinations. But don't be discouraged if and where you end up is not where you had planned it to be. Life has a funny way of helping you lay those bricks down a path much greater than you could have ever fathomed. That is the power of the Universe. And that is the power of taking the road less traveled — the one you create." – Me inspired by Will Smith and Robert Frost

I was watching a video one day of Will Smith being interviewed, and in it, he referred to this concept of "your wall."

Now let's first be clear; we are not talking about putting up a wall in your life to protect you from the world or to hide truths. It's not that kind of wall. Preferably in this context, the wall is going to be a destination, the masterpiece of life that you're trying to build.

And what we're getting at is it helps to have the vision of what the wall will look like. It doesn't need to be perfect, but it's helpful to have an idea. In our quote here, we talk about a path instead. Have an idea of what that path is going to look like, where it might be heading for you. But here's the kicker. You don't start with building that entire wall or path right away. No, it's going to take years and years.

Instead, have the idea of it, and then when you start, when you set out to build, you focus on laying that first brick and each one following as perfectly and as finely as you can arrange it. Focus on that one brick being placed so perfectly and so nicely, and then do the same for the next one, and then the next one, and then the next one. And sooner or later, you will have your path, your wall, or whatever it is you so choose to imagine.

I've recited this concept to many people before and have gotten a variety of unique substitutions. A flower garden. Plant each flower, beginning with the first, as nicely and beautifully as you can plant that one flower. Then the next one. And soon you will have your garden. The coolest part is that every single person's path, wall, or flower garden is going to look and be different. They'll be unique in their particular ways, and that's what makes us human.

Our lives are crafted, built, created in all different ways, and the essential idea to remember is to go about it *your* way. This is such a critical concept in the ability to balance and manage your life.

When one is time managed, one's time is most often balanced. Use the self-assessments that this book has provided to break down what it is that you're balancing in life.

Allocate the appropriate amount of time to each endeavor and stick to that even if it means removing some things. After all, you can't say yes to everything, and our friend, Warren Buffet, also reminds us that the most successful people say *"no"* more than anyone else.

We're limited to the number of hours each day, days in a week, and weeks in the year. So spend your limited time doing what you love and what it is that has a meaningful impact on your life. You're not expected to do everything and be everyone. We even discussed that people would pay more (money or their time) to those who do one thing extraordinarily well versus many things mediocrely. Time management is a significant key to balance.

It takes discipline to stick to a well time-managed schedule, especially with the number of distractions all around us. This is when it helps to have the daily schedule built days in advance, when you put the phone away while you're working, or simply hold yourself accountable at all times. Stick to it, and you will find your way, and even better yet, create your way.

MY GRANDMOTHER'S STORY

As I was drafting this very book, I was texting my grandmother, Anita Penn, hoping to include one of her hilarious yet enlightening stories. She was so proud I was finally pursuing becoming an author.

She and I shared an extraordinary life, and I will be forever grateful. From our nights of ice cream and Wheel of Fortune to Florida vacations and piano lessons, she was the greatest grandmother a grandson could ever hope for.

Unfortunately, her time with us was nearing, and we all, including herself, knew it. We were content, though. She was ready to join her husband, my grandfather, once again — as they'd been apart since his death in the Vietnam War. A single mother of three: two beautiful daughters and one handsome son. My mom, my aunt, and my uncle. Mary, JoAnn, and Charles (named after his father, my grandfather, our hero).

Rather than telling the story, I gained my mom's permission to include the eulogy she recently wrote for her. Yes, she is gone now. My grandmother was not able to stay with us long enough to share a story for this final chapter, but we're blessed to know it was her time, and that my mom is here to carry her legacy on.

This book and this final chapter are here to carry her legacy on. Her eulogy reads:

"How would I describe Mom? Well, SHE identified and often introduced herself as a 'widow with three kids.' But Mom was also Funny. Strong. Smart. Self-effacing. Approachable. Determined. Selfless. Hopeful. Beautiful and perfectly human. As Penn children, and throughout our entire adult life, our father was portrayed as a hero. A war hero. And he was. But Mom...She was brave. Full of courage. No training. No uniform. No awards. No medals. No ceremonies nor plaques as her reward or motivator to get through life's trials.

There weren't cell phones, Google, shortcut apps, or GPS trackers available as parental aids, but she did her best with what she had and what she thought was right. It wasn't until I became a mother did I realize a fraction of how many sacrifices Mom made for us kids. Last-minute book reports, missing the bus, tracking us down when we skipped school, boyfriend drama, getting us to our first high school jobs, midnight rescues when cars broke down, and the sleepless nights waiting for us to come home from a college party. Mom was the original Uber when it came to nightclub closing time. Many friends were loaded into that blue Econoline van after a night of dancing at Thursday's nightclub.

Mom never saw us Penn kids as the under-achievers in the Brady/Penn extended family tribe. We weren't the most book smart or the most ambitious, but she was proud of our kindness, our open-mindedness and generosity, our capacity to forgive, our willingness to re-move judgment of others, our adventurous — aka irre-sponsible — spirit to sometimes veer off life's path. Our flexibility to alter our course when life threw us a curve-ball we learned from Mom's example.

Mom assembled lawn mowers, learned how to repair pool filters, operated her own snowblower, fixed van doors when they fell off the track, and put in those window air conditioners after carrying them from the basement to the top floor (she told me to remember to mention that). She never complained about being alone, and as we know, raising three kids on Jackson Drive during our teen years was not the easiest or without drama and chaos. But she kept on us. Leaving night school early to intercept one of our rendezvous at the dead-end to catch us smoking. Or driving around local neighborhoods looking for us when the school alerted her we had skipped. As much as she knew this would not make her the 'cool mom,' she still ended up being the 'cool mom.' The house where everyone gathered during our high school and college years. Even welcoming some to live with us for a while.

If she made a mistake or a poor choice, her heart was always in the right place. She never squashed our momen-

tary fancies of VW bug convertibles, pink-painted bed-room walls, indoor roller-skating rinks in the basement where we spray painted the walls with graffiti. She'd let our passions run free when it came to re-decorating our bedrooms, or rearranging the garage so we could turn it into our stage for a Sound of Music revival or a go-cart and bike repair shop. Overcompensating for the lack of a father? Maybe. Is some 'misplaced guilt' for us not having grown up with a dad? Perhaps. Misguided efforts? Sure thing…Over-involved and codependent well into our present adulthood? Most likely a definite yes. Would I have wanted a mom any other way? Not a chance. I don't need to see a movie like 'It's a wonderful life' to know that Mom affected so many lives that crossed her path. A domino effect to enhance or enlighten lives beyond that singular person she touched. You didn't meet Mom and not leave without some laughs, greater insight into an-other culture, a juicy catholic school story from back in the day, or a desire to come back for more Momma Penn. She welcomed every one of our friends into our Jackson Drive home. No judgment. No question. She'd practiced all she learned from the Phil Donohue show or her night school social work classes on us kids and our friends. I can still remember her having us sit around the living room for hours well into the night until the fight whittled down to the bare bones, and the bottom line issue became evi-dent. She also made us do that one night until one of us fessed up to who ate the last Twinkie.

Mom never wanted anything for herself. Everything she did was for us. There were times I know Mom didn't have money for the basics, but we were never denied a prom dress, field trip money, or the tools needed to work on the newest used car. Tag sales on a spring weekend were one of my favorite alone times with Mom. We'd drive around in the van with our newspaper ads circled. Bonus if we came across a tag sale that wasn't advertised. We'd buy things we didn't need, just for the thrill of the bargain. She carried that habit right to the bitter end. 'I'm expecting a sympathy card from Lowes, Savers, Goodwill, Costco, and BJs.'

West Point road trips for cheap smokes, tax-free groceries, cat vaccinations, or a sore throat...it cost us extra in gas and a full day spent just for those few errands, but it didn't matter. West Point was her happy place, and I was the first to volunteer to be her ride-along. One of the few chances I ever got to beat out Jo for 'shotgun.' Standard practice was a box of Fig Newtons, one sleeve for me and one for her. An empty Tab can in the console cup holder and a two-liter bottle of diet soda for refills.

As a grandmother, she was very hands-on. Varence, Brady, Scarlett, and Connor kept her very busy and entertained. Mom would often take one or all for consecutive overnights in order to give us young parents a chance to regroup and have some adult time. Grandma Camp, she called it. She was instrumental in all four learning how to swim in her Lexington condo pool, getting school projects completed, introducing them to Broadway shows and museums in a way no school field trip ever could. Many trips to West Point, of course. She also had Scarlett be the documentary commentator on her camcorder for the groundbreaking of what is now the Lowes and AMC movie theater property. Why would someone do that?! Because Mom loved Danbury.

Last May 2019, during her pre-op evaluation for her heart surgery, Mom said, 'I'm concerned about the surgery. I don't want to lose any more weight.' We paused for a moment and then cracked up and let what she said sink in, and she then said: 'I didn't think I'd ever hear myself say those words!' Weight was a struggle for Mom, and in the end, it took her 'Florida diet' as she called it to finally feel excited about shopping for new capris, Tankini bathing suits, and, most recently, her Mother of the Bride

pink dress. Getting bathroom selfies from your 78-year-old mother in a tankini is something you just can't unsee.

Mom's original surgery date was in October 2018, so Bryon and I flew down to support her. Although the surgery was postponed we got to spend quality time together. Bryon installed her brick pavers with each kid and grandkid's name on it, then laid down sod and planted shrubbery in Mom's expert direction. One day at the community recreation area, she asked if I'd help her to the hot tub. Now mind you there were two tubs. One was in the shade and one was in the sun. There were three men in the sunny tub…older than me but younger than mom. I said to myself, 'Please God, let Mom choose the empty shady tub…these guys do not want some old lady of 78 with a cane and a tankini slinking in and invading their male bonding time.' Wouldn't you know it…she wants the sunny tub. These men helped her down the steps, and within minutes she had them in stitches talking about old stories from the Bronx and finding they not only knew some of the places she referred to but knew some of the family names she spoke of. Leave it to Mom to make friends anywhere she goes.

About two weeks ago, Mom and I were having an open, honest conversation about her final wishes. She said she was ready. She was tired and in pain. She asked if I was disappointed in her that she wanted to give up. That her older brother and sisters were still living full lives, and she, the baby, was losing hers and would I think of her as weak. She asked me to remind everyone that she had been strong her whole life and not to forget that.

I told her she still IS strong, and that letting go is a very brave and courageous thing to do.

Each of us Penn kids may have different memories or perceptions of how our story with Mom played out, but from this middle child's view, she was perfect, and I am proud to be my mother's daughter." – Mary Penn, The World's Most Loving Mother

Moral: *live*. Never stop living.

We are all blessed with this opportunity to live *one* life. Maximize every chance you get. Love every moment you can. There is no telling what exactly the Universe has in store for you, but it certainly is much more than you can ever fathom. And once you commit to this life of living, the Universe has a funny way of taking you by the hand.

EMBRACE YOURSELF

Above all else, *always* be yourself. No matter how cliche that might sound, it couldn't be any more accurate in all life's contexts. And in the context of this very book, being yourself is what's going to get you to that well-balanced life.

As we talked about in Chapter Twelve, take it all with a grain of salt. This book is not meant to tell you how to live your life. It's your life after all, and you should live it exactly how you like it. I encouraged you to be open-minded when you came into this book, and I genuinely hope that you have been throughout.

Someone once told me that the best learning could come from rubbing shoulders with the right person. This couldn't be truer — and what you've heard in this book has been years worth of just that.

> *"This above all: to thy own self be true."* – William Shakespeare, Poet, Playwright, and Actor

Balance is an art form, and once you think you've got it mastered, your life evolves. It develops because you reach a point in your life of such a well-achieved balance that you level up. You take the next step or leap in your life, and it's a whole new game of balance. That's precisely the way it's supposed to be.

There is no such thing as "figuring *it* out."

It isn't necessarily concrete. Sure, some people might have the "it" factor, so it's been called, but *it* is continuously changing and continuously growing at the end of the day. And we're frequently evolving, becoming a better version of ourselves.

That is the beauty of life.

Of growth.

Of opportunity.

Of significance.

"Only those who will risk going too far can possibly find out how far one can go." – T.S. Eliot, Poet, Essayist, Publisher, Playwright, Literary, and Social Critic

WRITE SOME NOTES

We did it. Well, *you* did it. I appreciate you.

Take this time for any thoughts on where to go from here. Not when to go, because that answer is yesterday. But *where* to go. I sincerely hope this book gave you a sense of direction by putting you in the driver's seat.

____

____

____

____

____

____

____

____

Get out there, get started, and keep going.

And *always* remember, *nobody* can stop you.

Chapter Fifteen.
Assessment Examples

Example A. (Credit to Karl Gibbons, TEMA):

90 Days to Accomplish - Next Checkpoint: _*Date*_

Start Three Things:

Stop Three Things:

Increase Three Things:

Decrease Three Things:

Example B. - Key Notes to Follow:

List Keynotes from each chapter's self-assessment

Example C. - Time Allocation:

Daily:
Weekly:
Monthly:
Quarterly:

Semi-Annually:

Annually:

Example D. - "NO" (12 to 15 Things)

List 12 or more things to say "no" to and refer back to this assessment to measure progress

Example E. - 5+ Year Scope:

List the next five years ahead and decide what role(s) you will be holding at that time

Example F. - Professional/Personal Goals:

List five to ten professional goals related to your career path and then five to ten personal goals related to your career path

Example G. - Books to Read:

1. *Who Can you Trust?*, Rachel Botsman
2. *Talk like TED*, Carmine Gallo
3. *E-myth*, Michael E. Gerber
4. *Talent Wins*, Ram Charan, Dennis C Carey, Dominic Barton, and Dennis Carey
5. *Rich Dad Poor Dad*, Robert Kiyosaki and Sharon Lechter
6. *Think and Grow Rich*, Napoleon Hill

7. *The Fourth Turning*, Neil Howe and William Strauss

8. *Talking to Strangers*, Malcolm Gladwell

9. *Quit and Get Rich*, Karl Gibbons

10. *Making Hope Happen*, Shane J. Lopez

11. *Zero to One*, Peter Thiel

12. *The Alchemist*, Paulo Coelho

13. *Outliers*, Malcolm Gladwell

14. *The Personal MBA*, Josh Kaufman

15. *The Subtle Art of Not Giving a Fuck*, Mark Manson

Bonus* My Next Book – Stay Tuned

Example H. - Solutions to Conflict of Interest:

1. Open Communication

2. Six Months Patience Period

3. Financial Stability for Minimum of Three Months

4. See the End; Create the Runway

5. Understand Responsibility

6. Analysis

7. Must Have Synergy

8. Identify Personal Mantra(s)

9. Make Decision When Most Afraid

10. Trust and Know Thyself

HONORARY ACKNOWLEDGMENTS

A very special and honorary *thank you* to a handful of people who have helped me get to where I am today.

To my entire family of Firmenders and Penns.

To Aunt Grace, who is not blood but cared for me as such.

To my other family, the DDF's, and my hometown of Danbury.

To my Coaches throughout Pop Warner and High School – Danbury Trojans and Danbury Hatters.

To my brothers, Tyler Walton, Kyle Williams, as well as my SWFL family.

To an extraordinary part of my life, Alyssa Enright.

To Florida Gulf Coast University, LeaderShape and FGCU's School of Entrepreneurship.

To my first business partner, Brenden Kelly, and VIIX Entertainment.

To Jakub Adamowicz and the RoomDig team.

To Natalie Finazzo and the Fieldr team.

To my proofreaders/editors Nolen Rollins, Cheryl Lampard, Robert Swensen, and Mathew Reyes.

To my incredible illustrator, Marena Sanoja.

To the anecdotal contributors in this book, Steven Becker, Geoff Evans, Ross Gibbs, Ashley DeBoer, Brandon Catron, Eric Gallus, Benjamin Fleischer, Karl Gibbons, Dr. Christopher Blakely, Dr. Sandra Kauanui, Dr. Kathleen Houlihan, and Nolen Rollins.

My gratitude spreads far beyond any list that I could put together. So to all of you reading and to all of those who support, I thank you and appreciate you sincerely.

May you all live the lives that you dream of.

THE

EVER-EVOLVING

ART OF BALANCE

CITATIONS

- Abbott, Brianna. "Youth Suicide Rate Increased 56% in Decade, CDC Says." *The Wall Street Journal*, Dow Jones & Company, 17 Oct. 2019, www.wsj.com/articles/youth-suicide-rate-rises-56-in-decade-cdc-says-11571284861.

- "About Tesla: Tesla." *Tesla, Inc*, www.tesla.com/about.

- Belasco, James A., and Ralph C. Stayer. *Flight of the Buffalo*. Grand Central Publishing, 2008.

- "BEST MOTIVATIONAL SPEECH BY ERIC THOMAS A.KA ET." *Success Learned*, 9 July 2019, www.successlearned.com/motivational-video/best-motivational-speech-by-eric-thomas-a-ka-et/

- "Bill Gates." *Biography.com*, A&E Networks Television, 4 Dec. 2019, www.biography.com/business-figure/bill-gates.

- Cherry, Kendra. "How Maslow's Famous Hierarchy of Needs Explains Human Motivation." *Verywell Mind*, Verywell Mind, 3 Dec. 2019, www.verywellmind.com/what-is-maslows-hierarchy-of needs-4136760.

- Collins, James C. *Good to Great*. Random House Business, 2001.

- *DailyOM*, www.dailyom.com/

- "Definitions for CONSTRUCTIVE CRITICISMCONSTRUCTIVE CRITICISM." What Does CONSTRUCTIVE CRITICISM Mean?, www.definitions.net/definition/CONSTRUCTIVE CRITICISM.

- "Destiny's Odyssey." *Destinys Odyssey*, destinysodyssey.com/personal-development/personal-development/personal-mantra/.

- "Effective Listening Is More Important Than Talking: 6 Secrets You Need to Know." *Work Smarter Stress Less*, 6 Dec. 2018, worksmarterstressless.com/listening-is-more-important-than-talking/.

- "EOS - Entrepreneurial Operating System for Businesses, Home of Traction Tools & Library." *EOS Worldwide*, www.eosworldwide.com/.

- Gallup, Inc. "StrengthsFinder 2.0." *Gallup.com*, Gallup, 30 Jan. 2020, www.gallup.com/cliftonstrengths/en/strengthsfinder.aspx.

- Gladwell, Malcolm. *Outliers: Why Some People Succeed and Some Don't*. Little Brown & Co., 2008.

- Harris, Marc Ashley. "The Relationship Between Physical Inactivity and Mental Wellbeing: Findings from a Gamification-Based Community-Wide Physical Activity Intervention." *Health Psychology Open*, SAGE Publications, 16 Jan. 2018, www.ncbi.nlm.nih.gov/pmc/articles/PMC5774736/

- "Home." *Destiny's Odyssey*, destinysodyssey.com/.

- MANSON, MARK. *SUBTLE ART OF NOT GIVING A F*CK: a Counterintuitive Approach to Living a Good Life*. NEWBURY House Publishers, 2019.

- Mcleod, Saul. "Maslow's Hierarchy of Needs." *Simply Psychology*, Simply Psychology, 20 Mar. 2020, www.simplypsychology.org/maslow.html.

- Michele, et al. "SMART Goals: – How to Make Your Goals Achievable." Time Management Training From MindTools.com, www.mindtools.com/pages/article/smart-goals.htm.

- Michele, et al. "The Wheel of Life®: – Finding Balance in Your Life." *The Wheel of Life - Time Management Techniques from MindTools.com*, www.mindtools.com/pages/article/newHTE_93.htm.

- *Monitor on Psychology*, American Psychological Association, www.apa.org/monitor/2019/03/trends-suicide.

- Moralstories. "The Four Smart Students • Moral Stories." *Moral Stories*, 8 Oct. 2019, www.moralstories.org/four-smart-students/

- Naeem, Hassan. "How I Plan to Become a Better Learner." Medium, Medium, 14 Apr. 2019, medium.com/@hassan.naeem101/how-i-plan-to-become-a-better-learner-5cba9e9ed04c.

- "Premiere Plus Realty." PREMIERE PLUS AGENT, naplesrealestateproperties.com/premiere-plus-realty/.

- Robbins, Tony, et al. "Tony Robbins, Dean Graziosi, Jenna Kutcher & Russell Brunson." *Tony Robbins, Dean Graziosi, Jenna Kutcher & Russell Brunson*, links.mastermind.com/a/2049/click/1806/843024/3da740c753953c3db617c978cf-b39d3d99783635/22876c477feffecbf70464eead-052dafdf7de4a4.

- "Serena Williams." ATHENA UNLIMITED, www.athenaunlimited.com/empowerher-blog/serena-williams.

- The Editors of Encyclopaedia Britannica. "Kobe Bryant." *Encyclopædia Britannica*, Encyclopædia Britannica, Inc., 26 Jan. 2020, www.britannica.com/biography/Kobe-Bryant.

- Thiel, Peter A., and Blake Masters. *Zero to One: Notes on Startups, or How to Build the Future*. Virgin Books, 2015.

- "Was Michael Jordan Really Cut from His High School Team?" *Yahoo! Sports*, Yahoo!, sports.yahoo.com/michael-jordan-really-cut-high-school-team-215707476.html.

- Wickman, Gino. *Entrepreneurial Leap: Do You Have What It Takes to Become an Entrepreneur?* BenBella Books, Inc., 2019.

- Wright, Christy, et al. "The Truth About Work-Life Balance." *Business Boutique*, 16 Apr. 2018, www.businessboutique.com/2018/04/the-truth-about-life-balance/.

- https://www.youtube.com/watch?v=C6KJB9r6vTo.

ABOUT THE AUTHOR

Connor Firmender
Entrepreneur, Author, Knowledge Broker
CoFounder & CEO of Fieldr
CoFounder of VIIX Entertainment
Creator of MotivatingTravel
FGCU School of Entrepreneurship Alumnus '19
Email: ConnorFirmender@gmail.com;
Info@FieldrInc.com
Website: ConnorFirmender.com
Follow Me on Social Media! @ConnorFirmender

Firmender graduated from Florida Gulf Coast University's School of Entrepreneurship, where he launched two startups — one in the entertainment industry and one in the software tech industry. While launching his startups, Firmender executively developed and grew a social startup, WearTheFund Apparel, where he managed a sales portfolio of over $1M and over 65 nonprofit partners, ultimately bringing the company to its first profitable year. His first startup, VIIX Entertainment, is an Event & Talent Management group, Independent Record Label, and managing partner of VIIX Studios, all based in Sarasota.

Firmender's latest success has been the launch of his software solution, Fieldr. Fieldr is a web-based software solution delivering career opportunities to students and emerging talent to employers. The focus is on bridging the gap in communication and career readiness between users through experiential learning and job opportunities. As the CEO of Fieldr, Firmender has a strong background in Sales, Marketing, Business Development, and Leadership Strategy.

He has also launched MotivatingTravel, a startup based in SWFL that coordinates and engages in social, cultural, and environmental initiatives. These initiatives include a global mission trip to mentor students and young professionals in underdeveloped regions of the world — beginning in Kenya, Africa, and efforts aiding the restoration of coral and marine life.

Firmender sits on the Legacy Leadership Forum, Career Advisory Boards for Lee County High Schools, Mentors for Collier County Public Schools NAF Academy, for LeaderShape, and is an Education Ambassador for Junior Achievement. Moreover, Firmender sits on an advisory committee for FutureMakers Coalition of SWFL.

Although his business endeavors play a significant role in the daily agenda, he prioritizes health and fitness through meditation and exercise. Giving back to his community is a priority, whether through volunteer engagement, service learning, or mentoring. In his entirety, Firmender anticipates being a serial entrepreneur, investor, and writing many books in the coming years.

He's recognized in Estero Life Magazine, Gulfshore Business, Business Observer, SWFL Business Today, FGCU EagleMedia, and SCORE. Connor has also been named the 2019 Southwest Florida SCORE Entrepreneur of the Year.

THE

EVER-EVOLVING

ART OF BALANCE

9 798625 735599